SACRAMENTAL AND OCCASIONAL HOMILIES

I

Sacramental and Occasional Homilies

David Q. Liptak

ALBA · HOUSE   NEW · YORK

SOCIETY OF ST. PAUL, 2187 VICTORY BLVD., STATEN ISLAND, NEW YORK 10314

Library of Congress Cataloging in Publication Data

Liptak, David Q.
  Sacramental and occasional homilies.

  1. Catholic Church—Sermons. 2. Sacraments—Sermons.
3. Occasional sermons. 4. Sermons, American. I. Title.
BX1756.L56S22   252'.02   80-29287
ISBN 0-8189-0408-9

Nihil Obstat
The Reverend Gene E. Gianelli

Imprimatur:
†John F. Whealon
Archbishop of Hartford
January 9, 1980

The Nihil Obstat and Imprimatur are
a declaration that a book or pamphlet is considered
to be free from doctrinal or moral error. It it is not implied
that those who have granted the Nihil Obstat and
Imprimatur agree with the contents,
opinions or statements expressed.

Designed, printed and bound in the United States of
America by the Fathers and Brothers of the
Society of St. Paul, 2187 Victory Boulevard,
Staten Island, New York 10314, as part of their
communications apostolate.

---

1 2 3 4 5 6 7 8 9 (Current Printing: first digit).

To Mary
Our Lady of Mount Carmel, and of
The Mountain of Brightness (Jasna Gora),
in the spirit of
Bernard of Clairvaux,
Albertus Magnus,
and Maximilian Kolbe
With an added prayer
of thanksgiving for
Pope John Paul II

Foreword

Having but recently worked on a homily plan to cover the three-year cycle of Sunday and Holy Day Scripture readings, I appreciate the special need to help priests and deacons with homilies for special occasions.

The homiletic challenge of the Catholic minister of the word goes far beyond Sundays and Holy Days. In most parishes, at least larger urban parishes, the weekly schedule calls for homilies in the presence of grieving relatives at a funeral, or with a married couple and their relatives and friends, or before the congregation as a sacrament is celebrated. These are all teachable, homiletic moments.

To have guidance towards the preparation of such occasional and sacramental homilies is no small blessing. Father David Liptak is practiced in pastoral and liturgical work, is skilled in writing and delivering homilies, and is a writer of lengthy experience.

Therefore to all interested in the art of developing homilies I warmly commend this new, welcome, book of Father Liptak.

Most Reverend John F. Whealon
Archbishop of Hartford

February 29, 1980

Author's Preface

Preaching the Gospel, the principal form of the ministry of the word of God, is a privileged obligation common to all those constituted in Holy Orders: bishops, priests or presbyters, and deacons. Vatican Council II reminds us that it is one of the primary responsibilities of priests and bishops. Preaching *draws* those who open their hearts to God, to his community, of which the bishop is the focal point of unity in Christ in a local congregation, where Christ is made present supremely through the reenactment of the mystery of the Eucharist, ''that by the flesh and blood of the Lord's body the whole brotherhood may be joined together'' (*Dogmatic Constitution on the Church*, sec. 21, 25, 26).

The highest actualization of preaching occurs in the liturgical homily, especially during the Eucharist.

Cardinal Augustine Bea, one of the great biblical minds of recent times and a leading light of Vatican Council II, once noted that the direct union between the proclamation and preaching of God's word with the sacrifice of the Mass is a phenomenon proper to Catholicism; it is thought to go back to the example of Christ at the Last Supper, who, before changing the bread and wine into his Body and Blood, prefaced his action with admonitions, consolations and instructions (*The Pastoral Value of the Word of God in the Sacred Liturgy*, from *The Assisi Papers*, Collegeville, 1957, pp. 76-77).

Preaching sets the stage for encountering Christ in the sacraments. Acts 2:14-42, for example, reads: ''And they were persevering in the teaching of the Apostles and in the Communion, the breaking of bread and in the prayers.'' Preaching is prior to liturgical celebration; it mysteriously helps occasion the desire for grace, without which there is no sacramental encounter. Without the ministry of the word, the ministry of the liturgical rite (e.g., Mass, Baptism, Penance) can be rendered unfruitful either through ignorance or lack of necessary dispositions.

Vatican Council II reaffirmed the Church's emphasis on the ministry of the word in liturgical celebration. The new rituals, for example, provide for a homily as part of the administration of the sacraments. This is especially true of the homily at Mass, which is recognized as "integral" to the Eucharistic rite. (Even in the early Mass described by St. Justin Martyr, the two parts of Mass, Liturgy of the Word and Liturgy of the Eucharist, were inseparable; the Eucharistic Prayer must follow upon Bible reading and the homily.)

The importance of liturgical preaching was recently restated by Pope John Paul II in his apostolic exhortation on catechetics, *Catechesi Tradendae*, made public on 25 October, 1979. In Section 48 of this important document we read:

> . . . Respecting the specific nature and proper cadence of this setting (i.e., the liturgy), the homily takes up again the journey of faith put forward by catechesis and brings it to its natural fulfillment. At the same time it encourages the Lord's disciples to begin anew each day their spiritual journey in truth, adoration and thanksgiving . . .
>
> Preaching, centered upon the Bible texts, must then in its own way make it possible to familiarize the faithful with the whole of the mysteries of the faith and with the norms of Christian living. Much attention must be given to the homily: It should be neither too long nor too short; it should always be carefully prepared, rich in substance and adapted to the hearers, and reserved to ordained ministers. The homily should have its place not only in every Sunday and feast-day eucharist, but also *in the celebration of baptisms, penitential liturgies, marriages and funerals.* This is one of the benefits of the liturgical renewal. (Italics added.)

The major portion of this book of 40 sermons contains homilies for various sacramental (e.g., Baptism) or special liturgical (e.g., First Communion) events. Since the ministry of the word encompasses certain nonliturgical events (e.g., Rosary devotions, ecumenical or interfaith meetings), several homilies for these are provided. Finally, a few sermons for occasional parish functions (e.g., the commissioning of catechists) and parish concerns (e.g., priestly or religious vocations) are included.

These brief homilies are meant primarily as models for further amplification and application. Preaching is, after all, a unique event. Liturgical scholar Dom Cyprian Vagaggini describes preaching as: ". . . the oral announcement of the message of God centered on the mystery of Christ, sacred history, or paschal mystery, made by the Church through her authentic ministers, to the community of the faithful . . . to induce them to respond to the vital exigencies which are the subject of the message" (*Theological Dimensions of the Liturgy*, Collegeville, 1976).

I should like to thank Reverend Anthony L. Chenevey, Editor of Alba House, for encouraging me to write these homilies, and Reverend Francis J. Lescoe, Ph.D., Chairman of the McAuley Institute of Religious Studies and Professor of Philosophy at St. Joseph College, West Hartford, Connecticut, for his advice regarding their content. A word of appreciation is also due to my sister, Sister Dolores Liptak, Ph.D., of St. Joseph College, for helping with the final editing; and to Mrs. Joyce Boudreau of the Catholic Transcript staff for typing the manuscript.

D.Q.L.

CONTENTS

PART I: THE SACRAMENTS

PART II: THE EUCHARIST

PART III: SPECIAL DEVOTIONS

PART IV: JUBILEES AND ANNIVERSARIES

PART V: ECUMENISM AND INTERFAITH

PART VI: PARISH OCCASIONS

PART VII: SPECIAL GROUPS, NEEDS AND TIMES

PART I

THE SACRAMENTS

For the Baptism of an Infant

(Mark 10:13-16)

We are here, representing the Christian community, to receive a child into Christ's Mystical Body, the Church, through Solemn Baptism.

The Gospel we have just read—from Mark's Gospel, the first Gospel chronologically—reveals that as Jesus would not bar little children from seeking his embrace, so we bring little children—infants—to sacramental encounter in the waters of Baptism.

Today's Gospel is especially pertinent to this occasion, because the verb, "hinder," in Jesus' words, "Do not hinder the little children" (the Greek *koulein*), is the same verb used in the early baptismal liturgy when, as today, some questioned whether it was proper—or even valid—to baptize infants.

There are some who still object to the practice of baptizing infants. The reason usually alleged is that the Bible views baptism as the sacrament of faith par excellence; hence, no one can receive baptism unless he or she has made beforehand an act of faith. Infants, who are incapable of eliciting personal faith, the objection concludes, cannot therefore be baptized.

As Catholics, we of course believe otherwise.

It is true that Scripture requires faith antecedent to any real sacramental encounter. But is *personal* antecedent faith always demanded of the one who makes the encounter?

Read Mark 2:1-12, the story of Jesus' healing the paralytic carried by his friends. The Gospel clearly states that the sick man was saved not precisely through his own faith, but by "their faith" (i.e., the faith of his friends). The original Greek leaves no doubt about this. Matthew and Luke also focus on the faith of the paralytic's friends.

Thus Scripture sets forth the doctrine of salvation by the *faith of the community*. Although there is a general rule that Christ's saving action is impeded without antecedent personal faith, occasionally the faith of others, of the community, is cited as the condition for salvation.

In the case of infant baptism, the believing Christian community, the Church, represented by the baptizing priest, the parents, godparents and witnesses,—you and I—supply in a sense the required dispositions of faith in behalf of the infant.

You and I therefore help to *supply* what this infant (these infants) cannot yet elicit or express: faith in Jesus as Lord: Jesus, the Son of God Incarnate who, having suffered and died for us, now *lives* as glorified risen Lord, to take us into his Mystical Body through the forgiveness of sins, and open the doors to his Father's Kingdom for us. This is the reason why we, in this baptismal rite, read the word of God; this is why, too, the parents and godparents renew their creedal stance.

We know that these infants must, when they arrive at the age of reason, ratify their baptismal vows—in first Holy Communion, for example—as we all did. But in the interim, it is our belief that God takes our word in trust, as it were, against that day of ratification.

Thus, we now intensify our faith-commitment. As we proceed with this ceremony, we are deeply aware of the necessity of entering into it prayerfully, with our hearts open to the Spirit's promptings.

And we continue to pray that the mystery which is unfolding before us now may grace a hundredfold the infants, N., N., N., whom we are about to bring to the baptismal font.

For (During or Prior to) Confirmation

Confirmation, or Chrismation, Cardinal Richard Cushing of Boston once remarked, is in a sense "the Cinderella of the sacraments, neglected and little understood." Yet confirmation ranks with baptism and the Eucharist as one of the three sacraments of initiation, and permanently configures the recipient closely to Christ through a "seal" or "character."

"Confirmation" mirrors a Latin word for "make strong;" "chrismation," another Latin derivative, pertains to holy chrism, used for anointing in the conferral of this sacrament. This anointing, which symbolizes bestowal of growth and strength through the Holy Spirit, occurs through "the laying on of the hand" of the confirming minister, usually a bishop. (Priests can confirm in need, and in certain other situations).

As baptism constitutes a new birth, confirmation strengthens the new life acquired by baptism. It is described as the sacrament of Christian maturity, corresponding to adulthood in the physical and psychological development of the person.

This does not mean however, that confirmation should be postponed until chronological maturity is achieved. Precisely because it is a sacrament of initiation, it can be conferred immediately after baptism, as is the case among Eastern Rite Catholics. In the Latin Rite in the United States, it is generally conferred in late childhood or in early adolescence. Since confirmation is a sacrament of growth, it must of course be received in the state of grace.

Confirmation relates to Pentecost, as baptism relates to the Resurrection. One way to explain this is to say that whereas in baptism we are immersed in the death and Resurrection of Christ, in confirmation we enter more fully into the graced mystery of the Spirit's coming on Pentecost Sunday.

Being signed with the Holy Spirit's gift in confirmation so thoroughly configures the baptized person to the image of the risen Lord, that it "seals" him or her permanently as gifted with Christ's spirit. The effect of this action is theologically described as a permanent character. This character, based on the Biblical seal (Greek: *sphragis*) with which God's elect are indelibly marked (*see* Rv 7:2-8), is interpreted by some theologians as a sign of God's fidelity. Thus, confirmation cannot be repeated. Once conferred, it, like baptism, cannot be repeated; its unique and permanent consecration, signaling God's fidelity, renders it permanent.

To encourage growth, a special set of charisms, known as the Gifts of the Holy Spirit, is conferred through confirmation. Growth is, after all, a *process*. These gifts, used rightly, result in the fruits of the Spirit. Recorded by St. Paul, they are: charity, joy, peace, patience, benignity, goodness long-suffering, mildness, faith, modesty, continency, and chastity (Gal 5:22-23).

Cardinal John Wright once observed: "In a way, confirmation might be thought of as a kind of ordination of the young layman or laywoman to a place in the total life of the Church, to a specific calling in the life of the Church."

For a Communal Penitential Rite

(With the Sacrament of Reconciliation)

We are met here to pray and reflect on God's mercy, to thank Jesus the Good Shepherd for searching us out to reconcile us with the Father, to ponder our sinfulness, and to prepare for an adequate, worthy confession in the Sacrament of Penance.

We are met because we are realists. Only realists can adequately appreciate sacramental confession. Escapists, dreamers and pretenders can hardly comprehend it fully.

To approach the Sacrament of Penance or Reconciliation, one must know himself or herself, and consequently, his or her sinfulness and moral frailty. And he or she must be a believer in the reality of Christ's saving action through the Church and priestly absolution.

What was the first command that Jesus voiced in his first recorded sermon? Was it not a command to repent? (Read Mk 1:14). Mark (the first of the Gospels, chronologically) tells us that after Jesus had submitted to John's Baptism and fasted in the desert for 40 days, he appeared in Galilee with the Good News of God: "This is the time of fulfillment. The reign of God is at hand! Reform your lives and believe in the Gospel!"

This same injunction was repeated by the Apostles in their preaching after Pentecost Sunday. We read in Acts 2:38, for instance: "You must reform and be baptized, each one of you, in the name of Jesus Christ, that your sins may be forgiven . . ."

"Repent" or "Reform your lives" implies a universal need. The mandate (actually an invitation in love, since Christ does not compel us even to his saving embrace) would not have been given by Christ—who is Wisdom personified—unless it were applicable to every human being born into this world (with the obvious exception of our blessed Mother, Mary).

It was this same Christ who once said—upon overhearing a slurring remark made to his disciples by the Pharisees—"People who are in good health do not need a doctor; sick people do . . . I have come to call, not the self-righteous, but sinners" (Mt 9:12, 13).

Is it even possible for a Catholic to understand the meaning of these words and at the same time not possess a deep love for the Sacrament of Penance by means of which our sins are literally taken away by the living Lord Jesus? He who now glorifies at the Father's right hand, still mediates for us?

And who but one who knows his sinful nature can appreciate the full meaning of the phrase "taken away" with reference to Christ's merciful forgiveness? To "take away" means to remove forever.

Do we not repeat, in every Mass, just before Communion time, the words of John the Baptizer to Jesus: "Lamb of God, you *take away* the sins of the world?"

Essential to one's salvation is a realistic sense of one's sinfulness, a sense of one's responsibility for guilt of soul.

This sense can be undermined or blunted in many ways: by repeated deliberate sin, for example, or by pride; or by inordinate rationalizing to "justify" proximate occasions of sin.

One undermining factor in our day is a false psychology that equates or confuses sin with emotional or mental illness. Sin is a deliberate offense against God; it results in real guilt. Emotional or mental illness is not the same as sickness of soul; in fact, culpability for sin can be diminished or erased by serious psychiatric disease. Real guilt for sin can only be taken away by Christ in the Church; especially by that merciful encounter with the living Lord that we call confession.

We now ready ourselves for this merciful encounter. To be forgiven we know that we must first confess all mortal sins committed since our last worthy confession; we must confess them in number and kind, as well as we can remember. Too, we must be contrite; in other words, we must be sorry for having offended God who is all good and deserving of all our love; we must detest the sins committed; and we must have firm purpose of amendment.

For a few moments now, we pause in thoughtful silence, as we await our turn to approach the Sacrament of Reconciliation.

For a First Communion (A)

One thing we can all say today, on the occasion of your First Holy Communion, is that children are very important to Jesus.

Sometimes children are made to feel unimportant; they are too small, some people say, and therefore shouldn't be trusted with important things until they've grown up—until they're at least in the seventh or eighth grade. You know that there are certain places in which you would not be especially welcome without accompanying adults—at a fine New York restaurant, for instance.

But Jesus doesn't think that you are unimportant. Remember that once, during our Lord's life here in this world, when he was walking through the countryside, a group of children wanted to go to him. What happened, though? Some of Jesus' followers were rather stern to these children—as some present-day librarians can be when children go into the adult section of the library out of curiosity to see what older people read. Some of our Lord's followers even tried to keep these little children who wanted to talk with Jesus from getting close to him. They may have thought that Jesus didn't want to be bothered with children.

How did Jesus react when he heard about this? He said—it's recorded right in the Gospel—for example: "Let the children come to me. Do not shut them off" (Lk 18:16). In other words, Jesus called for the children, blessing them by placing his hands upon them.

Why? Because God is love. The great God who made the heavens and the earth—the sun, and the planets, and the animals, and the oceans, and the trees, and everything including you and me—the great God who created the world is also the *loving God* who wants nothing but good for us.

The supreme sign that God loves us—the *best sign that he loves* us—is the Eucharist (Holy Communion, which you are about to receive this morning for the first time of thousands of times in your life).

Eucharist means gift. It is God's perfect gift to us, since it is God himself, as he has revealed himself to us most perfectly, in Jesus. When we receive Communion with belief, we (really and truly) receive Jesus into our hearts so that he can love us as he loved the children in the Gospel story we just recalled, *and* so that we can love him, as the children who wanted so much to see him in the same Gospel story loved him.

Here is a postscript for the parents of these children so loved by the Lord, and who are about to approach the Eucharistic table for the first time.

These children are signs of your own commitment to belief in God, to faith that life does have meaning and is not a meaningless corridor of no exits: they are signs of your own dedication to the core of the Christian premise; namely, that Jesus is Lord, Jesus *lives*, Jesus *intervenes* in our historicity, Jesus awaits us at the Omega Point of our own lives.

These children have been baptized and brought to this sacramental encounter because of your faith. Even at this point of your young lives as parents, you have accomplished something of surpassing value in the supernatural area; your witness to faith is incarnate.

God bless you and keep you for your fidelity.

For A First Communion (B)

It is no simple task to preach to the members of a First Communion Class, and to their parents and godparents as well. Actually there are three generations represented today, because many grandparents are here too (perhaps some great grandparents, also). Yet the difficulty touches upon one of the many inexplicable aspects of the wonderful mystery of Christianity; namely, that it speaks not only to all classes and to all intellects and to all races of people, but relates as well to all ages—from the child newly arrived at the age of reason to the person fully matured in life's experience.

A child can believe, hope, and love as meaningfully, in his or her own way, as another St. Thomas Aquinas. For God responds to a person's turning toward him insofar as that person's capacity allows.

In one sense, the kind of faith an adult has differs from the kind of faith he had as a child, or even as a teen ager. For one thing, maturity of years ensures faith's testing, in a complexity of varied concrete situations. For another, the passing of the years permits a deepening of faith through the rich nourishment of sacramental encounter and prayer: especially by means of frequent confession and communion, by daily Bible reading and by personal devotions. Too, the adult who believes has come to know experientially that his or her faith cannot be scientifically demonstrated, after the fashion of a mathematical proof or a laboratory experiment; on the contrary, faith transcends human equations by a mysterious process that yields personal certainty freely embraced with love.

Take the Eucharist, for which these boys and girls—your sons and daughters, or your grandchildren, or your nieces and nephews—are about to receive today for the first time. As children you and I believed with all our hearts that when we received the Eucharist we received our divine Lord truly present under the appearances of bread and wine, and that by this Bread of Life we would live in Christ and be transformed by him. Yet as adults now, we can look back into our history and identify concrete situations for which there was no other answer than to embrace Christ in the Eucharist—an answer that literally gave us new life enabling us to face the grey corridors in which we often found ourselves wandering in this vale of tears.

But our remarks here should also be addressed to the children who are about to receive our Lord Jesus in Communion for the first time. And so a few words just for you boys and girls, now.

What I have just said to your mothers, fathers, sponsors, grandparents, and all the other adults here, is that people, no matter what their size, are today recognized as important before God. You know, dear children, how it is at home sometimes when company comes for that special dinner. When you were very little, you sometimes ate before the dinner; sometimes, at the kitchen table. You were not ready for adult dinners then; maybe you did not really appreciate the fine linens and the polite manners. But then one day you were old enough to take your place at the dining room table at great family banquets. Why? Because you had learned your manners, you knew how to listen to the good conversation, and most of all, you knew at least the value of good food and conversation.

What is happening today is like this. You are now old enough for God-talk in a serious way; for good conversation. You know the rules for dining at the Communion Table of our Lord. And, most important of all, you know the value of the special spiritual nourishment you are about to take for the first time: the *Bread of Heaven*, Jesus himself. Today the Church recognizes that you can believe, trust, and love Jesus as truly as an adult can. So the Church invites you forward this day to dine at Jesus' own table.

God keep you always in his graces. And may he bless your good parents who have brought you to this glorious moment. And your grandparents and godparents, too. We all remember how beautiful a day it was for us, when we, like you, made our *first* Holy Communion.

For a First Communion (C)

Girls and boys, parents, relatives, and friends of these girls and boys who are about to make their first Holy Communion.

I know some things about this first Communion class. For one thing, I know that you like to hear stories. Also, I know that you like to draw—with crayons, for instance. Well, there is a story about a girl—about the same age as you first communicants—who also liked to draw with crayons.

One day this girl said to her mother: "I'm going to draw a picture of God."

"Of God?" her mother asked. "You can't do that because no one knows what God looks like."

The little girl answered: "When I'm finished with my drawing, everyone will know what God looks like."

Now I don't want to get into any trouble with the mothers here, but the little girl was right. The fact is that we can know what God looks like, exactly what he looks like. We *can* take up a crayon and paper and draw a perfect picture of God.

How? Because God told us what he looks like when he made himself known to us in Jesus. God looks like Jesus. To know what God looks like, how God acts, what God does; we have simply to look at Jesus Christ.

Look at Jesus then. What is the first thing that comes to mind when we see Jesus, or listen to his words? The first thing? It's love; correct? Jesus shows us that God is love.

Look at Jesus, inviting the little children to come to him. Look at Jesus, feeding the thousands of people who were hungry. Look at Jesus, forgiving sinners. Look at Jesus, giving sight to blind people, curing the diseased, letting lame people throw away their crutches and walk, raising dead people back to life. Yes, God shows himself to us in Jesus Christ, and Jesus is love.

Which brings up another topic, which we could direct to your wonderful parents. If God reveals himself in Jesus, and Jesus is love, you must always be careful to teach *this* to your children, and to stress it.

A woman columnist of national reputation once wrote about seeing a small boy grinning in church. He wasn't humming, or tearing pages out of hymnals, or kicking his feet against the pews. The little boy was just smiling.

Suddenly, the columnist wrote, the child's mother spun the boy toward her, and in a "stage whisper" that could be heard off Broadway scolded, "Stop that grinning, you're in Church!"

The mother backed up her words with a touch of corporal discipline. When the child began to cry, she added, "That's better." Then *she* returned to her praying.

The columnist said she wanted to "grab this child" and tell him all about *her* God, a happy God, a smiling God, the God who even understands a mother's prayer, "If you can't make me thin, then make my friends fat" (Erma Bombeck, in The Hartford Times, Feb 27, 1970).

Of course. Christianity is a religion of joy. God is kindness personified. God, Scripture tells us, is love.

This of course is the primary meaning of the Eucharist, which these children here today are about to receive for the first time. God so loves us that he invites us to his table to share in his own life with the Father.

And to this banquet, in his love, he calls children—as this beautiful celebration witnesses.

For the Anointing of the Sick

(Anointing of the Sick During Mass or in a Communal Rite)

Job 19:23-27a (Ritual, No. 157)
James 5:13-16 (Ritual, No. 178)
Matthew 11:25-30 (Ritual, No. 207)

We are gathered here in faith, fully aware that, as today's Gospel from Mattthew reveals, Christ the living Lord can help us shoulder the burdens of illness or advanced age in a blessed manner.

It is our Catholic faith that the Sacrament of the Anointing of the Sick was instituted by Christ for the benefit of those who are ill. One of the Biblical witnesses to this Sacrament is today's Second Reading, James the Apostle's classical invitation to the sick to call in the priests—the presbyters—of the Church that they might be anointed in the name of the Lord with a prayer made in faith toward the forgiveness of sins and restoration of health. Here James doubtless had in mind something he had experienced long before Jesus' Resurrection. We read, (Mk 6:13), that he and the other Apostles in response to the Lord's directions, preached, expelled demons, "anointed the sick with oil, and worked many cures."

The Anointing of the Sick—also known as Extreme Unction—is viewed by the Church, which reads the Bible with the infallible assistance of the Holy Spirit, as an opportunity for encountering the healing Savior during the hour of serious illness. Dangerous illness resulting from disease or advanced age is what this means; the presumption is that health has been lost through internal causative factors, factors intrinsic to the person. Hence, to be anointed, one must be seriously sick. (A prudent or probable judgment concerning the gravity of the sickness suffices). If a dangerous illness is the reason for planned surgery; then, again, the person not only can, but should be anointed, prior to the surgery. Old persons may be anointed if they are in weak condition, even though no dangerous illness is present. And sick children may be anointed if they have sufficient use of reason to be comforted by the sacrament.

One could emphasize here that the right time to request to be anointed is when one *begins to be in danger* from sickness or old age.

What condition of soul is required for this sacrament? Our faith is that Extreme Unction is a sacrament of the living; the state of grace is therefore required.

Specifically, what happens in the sacramental encounter for which we are now assembled? What happens is this: by virtue of the anointing, the sick person's illness is mysteriously immersed into Jesus' Passion and Death. By the grace conferred, the anointing takes away sins, if any remain to be taken away, together with the remnants of sin. By this grace, too, the soul of the sick person is relieved and strengthened; and great confidence in the divine mercy is aroused. As a result, the one anointed "may more easily bear the trials and hardships of his sickness, more easily resist the temptations of the devil 'lying in wait' (Gn 3:15) and sometimes regain bodily health, if this is expedient for the health of the soul" (*Apostolic Constitution, The Sacrament of Anointing of the Sick*, issued by Pope Paul VI, 30 November, 1972).

In today's First Reading, Job, in the midst of physical suffering and depression, cries out in belief, "This I know: that my Savior lives." Job, however, could not even dream of what for us is a reality; namely, the risen Lord Jesus, the Son of God Incarnate, saying to us, in the depth of *our* agony as serious illness or advanced age weakens us: "Come to me, all you who labor and are overburdened . . . and you will find rest for your souls . . ."—today's Gospel.

If we receive this Sacrament of the Sick in sincere and intense faith, we *shall* hear these words spoken to us by the same loving Lord, who comes to us across the years, with his healing, strengthening embrace.

For a Nuptial Mass

Tobit 7:9-10, 11-15 or
Sirach 26:1-4, 13-16;
Ephesians 5:2, 21-23;
John 2:1-11

We are, here in this church dedicated to . . . , to celebrate a joyous event: a Christian wedding—a special Christian wedding, I could say. We are all here today because we know and admire this couple about to be married in Christ. We genuinely desire for them only the best, which surely means, in the first instance, the choicest of God's blessings.

In rejoicing on this occasion, however, we must also ponder its basic significance—its deepest meaning in faith. This event provides us with an opportunity in grace—to reflect upon the mystery of Christian marriage: a real, interpersonal encounter between the living Lord Jesus and the wedded couple.

For us, marriage is not simply a holy contract. The ancients instinctively sensed the sacredness of the marital bond. In pre-Christian Rome, for example, when a woman was given in wedlock, she literally had to be carried over the threshold enshrined with her father-in-law's household gods—the *manes, lares* and *penates*: and then solemnly initiated into her father-in-law's religion of the hearth. She was not permitted to enter into the religion of her new household on her own. Having touched the hearth fire of her husband's home, the bride was then invited to share the wedding cake with her husband; this too was a religious rite. Modern customs are reminiscent of these ancient rites.

In Old Testament Israel, God's Chosen People, aided by Revelation, advanced in the knowledge of marriage's covenanted sanctity. The Book of Tobit, for example, provides us with a beautiful, highly spiritualized picture of marriage and home life, based on and overflowing with, faith and prayer. Therein, in the young married's wedding prayer—the seventh and eighth chapters (part of which we read for our first Bible Reading)—it is stressed that real evil cannot harm a couple who enter wedded life with a sincere awareness of the holiness of marriage. [The Book of Sirach (today's First Reading) likewise focuses on the special holiness of the married state].

When Christ came, however, marriage took on an entirely new, never-dreamed-of-before, nobility. With Christ, marriage was raised to the stature of a covenant with the Son of God Incarnate.

One way to explain this doctrine is as follows: Christian marriage is not only a consecration of a man to a woman, and of a woman to a man, but also a true consecration of the wedding itself of a man and a woman made one, in a covenant with the risen and living Christ Jesus.

For anyone who calls upon the name of Jesus, marriage is neither defined simply in terms of a contract between husband and wife, nor only in terms of a holy event. It is truly a covenant with Christ; an agreement into which Christ enters, and pledges to remain. This is why we say, in Catholic theology, that it takes three to get married: the husband, the wife, and the living Christ.

Jesus, as today's Gospel about the marriage at Cana reminds us, chose to perform his first public sign at the celebration of a marriage; an earthly union so festive that the wine ran out. By this miracle Jesus foreshadowed another banquet, the one over which he presided on the first Holy Thursday in the Upper Room, when he changed not water into wine, but wine into his very presence: the Eucharist, given to us by his sacrificial death on the morrow.

Since that time, Christ wills to be present at every wedding feast; again, not to change water into wine, but to join with a couple through his eucharistic presence in a covenant that is real, dynamic, and enduring.

In joyous thanksgiving and humble prayer, we now celebrate the rite by which this covenant is sealed. With the bride and the groom we are mindful that we are at the threshold of an awesome mystery.

For a Mass of Christian Burial (A)

We are gathered for this Eucharist on the occasion of death, for which our Christian faith alone provides basic, adequate answers.

For St. Paul, writing with the Holy Spirit's guidance, death meant to go home and to be with Christ forever (Ph 1:23). Thus we know in faith that death is not the end, but only the beginning; that, in fact, no one who believes in Christ can ever really die.

St. Augustine, the great Doctor of the Church, wrote in the beginning of his *Confessions*, one of the world's most beloved books: "You made us for yourself, O Lord, and our heart is restless until it reposes in you." This is why the death day of Christian martyrs is traditionally called their real birth day. This is why we can speak of the funeral liturgy as a celebration, and why white vestments may be used.

This is not to deny that death is tragic; or that bereavement, which all of us here are now experiencing, is not dificult. Death, whenever it intervenes, is always shocking. It entails loneliness, mental and emotional suffering, spiritual questioning, physical pain, cultural rejection, separation.

Bereavement is likewise agonizing. It means being separated from a loved one, a person upon whom our lives were oriented, an individual by means of whom we tended even to understand and define our very selves. It can also mean the grief of having mysteriously participated in another's dying process, perhaps through keeping vigil over weeks or months.

But, again, our faith helps us overcome the sorrow that death and bereavement bring about. We grieve, as Mary Magdalen wept at the tomb of Jesus, as Jesus himself wept at the grave of Lazarus. Christ our Lord wept at death reminding us that grief is a perfectly Christian reaction to the tragedy of death. But we do not grieve as persons without hope. Our faith reminds us that—as St. Ignatius of Antioch said as he prepared for his own martyrdom: "It is better for me to die in Christ Jesus than to be king over the ends of the earth."

The faith on which we rely—the faith that helps us overcome the tragic aspects of death—is fundamentally faith in the risen Lord Jesus, symbolized by the Easter Candle here at this Mass. In Jesus, who conquered death and now lives, we too are called to resurrection and eternal life. As Jesus has risen from the grave and now *lives*, so everyone who believes in Jesus as Lord will surely rise and live forever. St. Paul tells us this clearly in his First Letter to the Corinthians.

At this Mass of Christian Burial we are praying for one who has believed in Jesus as Lord. Baptized into Christ's Body, N. (here mention the deceased by name) lived a life of faith, hope and love, in witness and sacrificial suffering service after the pattern set by Christ, and hence now merits the reward Christ promised to those who followed him. An exemplary member of this parish for . . . years, he (she) implemented his (her) belief in his (her) family, neighborhood and beyond, demonstrating a solid commitment always to the reality of the risen Lord Jesus in his (her) life and that of his (her) family (wife, husband, children), neighbors and all he (she) encountered. As friends or relatives of N. (the deceased), we acknowledge that we have been graced by him (her), that we have learned from him (her), and that we thank God for having known him (her). And we pray that the reward of heavenly life, which Jesus promised to all who keep faith, will be his (hers) without delay.

We pray this through Jesus Christ our Lord. Amen.

For a Mass of Christian Burial (B)

We are here to celebrate a Mass of Christian Burial for N., who has gone home to be with Christ—as St. Paul defines death (Ph 2:23).

"To *celebrate* a Mass of Christian Burial," we say.

Death is of course shocking, the most shocking event in human life. We do not pretend otherwise. Bereavement is likewise shocking. We know this too, but we are not afraid to face it. Death and bereavement mean sorrow and separation and loneliness and all kinds of anxieties. Yet, as St. Paul reminds us, we do not grieve as those who have no hope (Th 4:13).

As Christians we know that anyone who believes in Christ never really dies; that anyone who believes in Christ, will, after this brief interval we call death, rise with Christ through the power of his Resurrection.

Christ's earthly death, which seemed the end, was actually the beginning. Having conquered death, he brings to life forever those who die in him. Moreover, he or she who dies in Christ is assured of participating in the resurrection of the flesh on the last day.

This most comforting doctrine of our faith is symbolized by the Easter Candle which we see standing here before us. This Candle is a clear and forceful reminder that death can be adequately understood only with the illumination of Christian faith.

During the Easter Vigil this past year, while this church was in darkness, this Candle was blessed with new fire, solemnly carried down the aisle, and then placed before the altar. There the deacon or minister stood before it, and in song recalled the first Easter:

"This is the night when Jesus Christ broke the chains of death and rose triumphant from the grave.

"What good would life have been for us had Christ not come as our Redeemer."

Later, during the Easter Vigil ceremony, this Paschal Candle was plunged into the font of water being blessed for baptism, as a sign that by Christ's rising we rise to a new life in baptism—a life that will never end—if we keep faith.

The mystery of our baptism through waters quickened by Jesus' death and Resurrection is also recalled in this funeral Mass by the use of holy water, with which we have sprinkled the body of N. At that time our prayer was, that just as we died with Christ in baptism, so, through the same sacrament, we are destined to rise again with him (as the Easter Candle, plunged into the baptismal font during the Easter Vigil rite, was quickly drawn out and raised aloft).

Again, though, this destiny of Resurrection in Christ is assured only for those who keep faith, symbolized by the white pall being used here today. This pall represents the white baptismal vestment of grace, now seen as a pledge of glory.

We thank N. for his (her) witness to Christ. We thank God for having known N.; for having had the privilege of learning from him (her), or sharing his (her) faith, hope and love in Christ. (Here some words relating to details of the deceased's life may be appropriate; for example, his or her example as a parent or as a parishioner.)

In our faith we pray today that the light of faith in which N. walked the paths of this life might illuminate our ways—the symbolism of this Easter Candle again—so that we too might merit to be with Christ forever in our real homeland.

We pray too that *our* light of faith may burn brightly, not fitfully or dully, like a flickering candle in the dark recesses of a night shelter. With God's grace we too can be *beacons*.

For a Mass of Christian Burial (C)

Today we are gathered for worship on the occasion of a death.

From one viewpoint, death marks the final, free commitment at a close of a series of free commitments made during life.

God has entrusted us with the capacity to make of ourselves what we want to be for all eternity. From the first days of human awareness, we know that we are at liberty to choose for God—*for* our Christian values—or *against* God. For example, every time we freely choose to assist at Sunday Mass, we advance in our pilgrimage Godward; and, on the other hand, every time we elect not to participate in Sunday worship, we turn away from the God who loves us and calls us, in our freedom, to be with him forever.

As long as we can remember, we have been making such choices, and, consequently, gradually maturing in the life of grace. Such choices—commitments, really—were made when we determined to make a good First Communion, when we decided to go to confession regularly, when you insisted that you would marry in the Church, and so on.

In a sense, human existence is structured on a series of commitments. To be a Christian means to make firm choices. Our life can be described as a pilgrimage of steps toward God—or away from God.

Death is the final, free choice in life's pilgrimage Godward. The end of a journey consciously and freely taken with the Lord Jesus at one's side, it is one's eternal ''birthday,'' a birth day not imposed by circumstances (as in the case of one's entrance into this world), but freely realized as the supreme crowning moment in a series of commitments taken in life, from the first moments of moral activity. This is why St. Paul, writing to the Philippians, could describe death in terms of finally going home in order to be with Christ forever (Ph 1:23).

Why, though, must *death* intervene before we can depart and be with the Lord forever? Why couldn't it be that our final commitment in freedom as a sign of our love for God could be accomplished another way?

Here we approach the frontiers of a deep mystery of faith. For it is only from Revelation that we know for certain about the universality of death; that, in other words, all men will surely die. Biology cannot tell us as much. Revelation alone is the final word here. And Revelation—the Bible as read within the Church—not only tells us that each and every human being must die, but that death is a result of sin, in which all human beings—except Mary the Mother of the Lord—share (Rm 5:12; Heb 9:27).

What is important here is that death, whatever its ultimate course, and despite its pain, can be rendered beautiful through faith. For in faith, again, it can constitute the final test in a series of tests freely assumed in Christ, and, as such, can be one's eternal birth day.

This is why we as Christians can *celebrate* death simultaneously as we mourn it. This is why we can *celebrate* this Mass of Christian burial for N., while at the same time grieving for our loss. For we here recall the witness of a person who, as a faithful disciple of Christ, has throughout his (her) days made the pilgrimage of faith Godward through a series of commitments freely made. (Commitments made at marriage, during parenthood, in so many parish activities, etc. . .)

St. Hugh of Avalon, the 12th century French monk whom England's Henry II summoned to head a monastery he had established (in partial penance for his complicity in the murder of St. Thomas Becket), used to say: "What an awful thing if we could never die." Certainly this is a more realistic Christian attitude than its contrary, namely: "What an awful thing to die."

Death for a Christian is of itself, and despite its character of penalty for sin or its pain, a final test of love; the supreme option in a series of options freely made with love.

It is a beautiful thing to die in Christ.

For a Mass of Christian Burial (D)

We are assembled here at the Mass of Christian Burial for N.

In one sense this is a sad event. Our souls are sorrowful; there is a tendency to weep. But, sometimes we are tempted to ask, is it proper that we grieve so, that we weep so?

St. Augustine, one of the Church's greatest saints and theologians, asked these same questions on the occasion of his mother Monica's death. (She was a saint too, and had literally led her son Augustine to conversion). In his diary, one of the world's best loved books, known as *The Confessions*, Augustine admitted that at first he had consciously held back the tears of sorrow. Even during the funeral, he wrote, he did not think it fitting to weep, for his mother did not die unhappy, nor did she really die. But when the funeral was over, he set free the tears which he had repressed, spreading them beneath the Savior's compassionate heart. His mother Monica was surely with God and eternally happy now, but Augustine her son had suffered a loss. He was weeping for his own plight. He wrote:

". . . I set free the tears which I had repressed, that they might flow at their will, spreading them beneath my heart; and it rested in them, for Thy ears were nigh me . . ." *(The Confessions,* in *Basic Writings of Saint Augustine,* ed. Whitney J. Oates, New York: Random House, 1948, p. 144).

In another part of his *Confessions* Augustine explained that funeral rites are meant primarily to comfort the living in their sorrow of loss.

Thus grief can be *good.* Grief can not only be a truly human reaction to bereavement, but an entirely Christian response to the shocking experience of another's death.

In the Acts of the Apostles, that inspired history of the early Church, we read that after the martyrdom of St. Stephen, who was stoned to death for the faith, the disciples buried him "bewailing him loudly as they did so" (Ac 8:2). And following the death of the beautiful convert Tabitha, who used to sew for the early Christian community (her Greek name was Dorcas), we read that all the widows approached St. Peter with news of her death "in tears" (Ac 9:36-42).

Mary of Bethany is a key model for the Christian in mourning. Like Mary, we too weep for the loss of a partner, or a brother, or a daughter, or a friend. (Didn't Jesus himself weep at the grave of Lazarus?) Like Mary, too we are tempted to think that had the Lord been present, he could have "saved" the deceased for whom the funeral is conducted. It is only in unreserved faith, hope, and love that we, in the footsteps of Mary, come to the realization that Christ is the Lord of life who, by his conquest of death on the cross, calls us to him from before the empty tomb of Easter Sunday morning. Hence we know that anyone who believes in Christ will never really die.

Each time blessed water is used at a funeral—as it is used today—we are reminded that anyone baptized in Christ who kept his (her) baptismal commitment—as N. has done—can never really die, and will surely rise one day again with the living Lord Jesus.

Despite our very human sorrow today, therefore, for the loss we have experienced in the death of N., this unique person who has enriched our lives so much with his (her) witness (Here cite some examples of witness; e.g., parenthood, parish leadership, a loyal and persevering confession of faith), we do not grieve as persons without hope.

Faith, we know, erases the tragedy of death. Faith in Jesus can render death beautiful. Death and bereavement can be celebrated as well as mourned. For, again, despite the pain and separation that death entails, to die really means—for a Christian—to go home and be with Christ forever (Ph 1:23).

For a Mass Following Priestly Ordination (A)

("First Solemn Mass")

We are met today for what was once commonly called a "First Solemn Mass" of a newly ordained priest. It is not really a "first Mass," for a priest's first Mass is his ordination Mass, which he concelebrates with the ordaining bishop.

In a sense, though, the traditional descriptive is quite apt. The "solemnity" pertains to all of us, who are privileged to join in this special Eucharist marking not only the ordination of another priest, but also marking the ordination of this particular priest, Father N., whom we all personally know and love.

Ordained ministry—the priesthood or presbyterate—is, we believe, a faith concept since it constitutes a participation in Jesus' one, eternal Priesthood. It cannot be discussed without conscious reference to faith in God, in Christ, and in Christ's Church. Priesthood, Vatican Council II reaffirms, is a "service of Christ," "a service of" unceasingly building up the Church on earth into the People of God, the Body of Christ, and the Temple of the Holy Spirit" (*Decree on the Ministry and Life of Priests*).

Priesthood, therefore, does not transcend the Church; rather, it constitutes service *within* the Church; a service defined primarily in terms of Biblical preaching, of presiding at the Eucharist, and of sacramental leadership.

Priesthood, we also know, is permanent, since it confers a seal or character that cannot be effaced. This character is a reminder that Christ has irrevocably associated the Church with himself for the world's salvation. The presbyter therefore is a lasting sign that God's word will never be withdrawn.

As the Third Synod of Bishops expressed the foregoing:

"The priest is a sign of the divine prevenient plan which is today proclaimed and effective in the Church. He makes Christ, the Savior of all men, sacramentally present among his brothers and sisters in both their personal and social lives. He is a guarantor of the first proclamation of the Gospel for the assembling together of the Church, and also of the ceaseless renewal of the Church which has already been assembled. If the Church lacks the presence and activity of the ministry that is received, by the laying on of hands with prayer, she cannot have full certainty of her fidelity and of her visible continuity" (*The Ministerial Priesthood,* 1971).

Reflecting on this occasion thus, one conclusion is inescapable; namely, the need to appreciate priests. Pope John Paul II, addressing the priests of Rome on November 9, 1978 said it this way:

"We are necessary for men, we are immensely necessary, and not part-time, not half-time like 'employees'!"

Our Holy Father returned to this theme in his Holy Thursday Letter to Priests in 1979. Therein he recalled the situation of Iron Curtain countries of this world, where Catholics meet underground to pray, but are without the Eucharist. Pope John Paul wote:

> . . . Think of the places where for many years, feeling the lack of . . . a Priest, they do not cease to hope for his presence. And sometimes it happens that they meet in an abandoned shrine, and place on the altar a stole which they still keep, and recite all the prayers of the Eucharistic liturgy: and then, at the moment that corresponds to the transubstantiation a deep silence comes down upon them, a silence sometimes broken by a sob . . . so ardently do they desire to hear the words that only the lips of a priest can efficaciously utter. So much do they desire Eucharistic Communion, in which they can share only through the ministry of a priest, just as they also so eagerly wait to hear the divine words of pardon: *Ego te absolvo a peccatis tuis!* . . . Such places are not lacking in the world.

Today, then, we are met for appreciation—appreciation for the priesthood, appreciation for Father N., newly ordained for our Church. We thank God for him. We congratulate him and his family (parents, sisters, brothers). We wish him Godspeed in his priestly pilgrimage of life. And we here ask the Lord of the Eternal Harvest to send others like him, for us, as Jesus asked us to do.

For A Mass Following Priestly Ordination (B)
("First Solemn Mass")

We are met here solemnly to rejoice with a newly ordained priest, a priest whom we all know and love, Father N., who entered the Order of Presbyter last (date). We rejoice too with his family (his mother, father, sisters, and brothers), and we thank the Lord that they especially have been granted to see this beautiful day.

Ordination is an amazing grace. St. Paul's words to Timothy are especially meaningful to a priest: "I thank Christ Jesus our Lord, who has strengthened me, that he has made me his servant and judged me faithful ... the grace of our Lord has been granted me in overflowing measure, along with the faith and love which are in Christ Jesus" (1 Tm 1:12, 14).

As in the case of every priest, ordination constitutes Christ's last great word uttered in his life; Christ's crucial, irrevocable invitation. Whatever has followed in this earthly existence has only been a response to, a living out of, this ineffable, personal summons.

No one is worthy of Holy Orders. Christ accepts his priest as worthy only because Christ makes his priest worthy. Christ's call cleanses; his grace and strength supply what a human being called to his ministry cannot offer. The one called by Christ only need respond, as Isaiah did when invited to prophesy: "Here I am; send me!" (6:8).

No one seeks the priesthood on his own. Christ chooses his priests. He calls them through his Body, the Church, founded on Peter and the Apostles. He singles them out to witness to his word, to renew his eternal sacrifice, to dispense his grace.

Holy Orders brings to focus all else in one's existence. "The priest's life," theologian Karl Rahner explained, "must be invested with his vocation; and his vocation must remain no less his life though he be no longer able to exercise it in the civil sense, just as a musician in the original and one in the derivative sense are distinguished by the fact that the one is a musician because he lives by it and the other remains a musician even though he starves by it" (*Servants of the Lord*, p. 112).

The priest is not merely a religious functionary who performs certain tasks assigned to cult and teaching. In the priest, person and office merge into the mystery of the living Christ, the eternal High Priest (Heb 3:8).

A priest has no private life isolated from his calling. If the priest tries to separate his office from his life, by, for example, trying to keep himself for himself, while rendering the Church only specified duties that can be listed in a forty-hour week, he has violated his vocation. As Rahner notes, one can only fulfill priesthood by paying one's life for the privilege.

Priesthood today puzzles a world caught up in a secularist mentality as a result of which Transcendence—all God-talk—is artificially bracketed out of reality. Thus, one thanks God especially for being a priest *now*, when being a priest is not readily understood, and when it is more evident than ever before that the priest is but an unprofitable servant whom the Lord nonetheless never forsakes.

An occasion such as this solemn Mass reminds us to renew our appreciation for the priesthood, instituted by Christ to minister his word and his grace until he comes again; and to thank him especially for this particular priest, Father N., who has so confidently and hopefully responded to his call with the answer: "Here I am; send me!"

This is also an occasion to pray specifically for Father N., as well as all the priests to whom we are indebted, for thus responding to the Lord's call.

Mary, Queen of Priests, please pray for Father N., and for all priests. We ask this through Christ, our Lord, the Eternal High Priest of the New Testament, in whose priesthood the Church's ordained ministers share.

PART II

THE EUCHARIST

The Sacraments

For a Eucharistic Holy Hour (A)

(Ruth 1:16-19; 2:1-9; Matthew 14:14-21)

For the first Scriptural reading during this Eucharistic celebration, we listened to a passage from the Old Testament Book of Ruth, surely one of everyone's favorite books of the Bible.

The story of Ruth and her mother-in-law, Naomi, is especially beautiful.

Ruth, remember, was not an Israelite by birth. Rather, she was a foreigner, a Moabite. Her mother-in-law, Naomi, however, was from Bethlehem, though she had married a Moabite, and had moved to Moab. Naomi's husband had died, and Ruth's husband had also died. The two women, Naomi and her daughter-in-law, Ruth, found themselves widows—which in ancient times, when women could not work outside the home, and when there was no social security or insurance protection, was especially tragic. Naomi, we read, decided to go back to Bethlehem (where Jesus was later born), and Ruth insisted on going with her. Ruth pleaded:

"Do not ask me to abandon or forsake you! For wherever you go I will go, wherever you lodge I will lodge, your people shall be my people, and your God my God" (1:16).

Thus, the women returned together to Bethlehem. To exist from day to day, they asked permission to glean in a rich man's fields; his name was Boaz. From early morning until late in the evening, they would follow the reapers who gathered and bundled the wheat, in order to salvage a few stray fragments of wheat. They literally existed on these fragments.

Boaz, it turned out, was distantly related to Ruth. When he recognized her, he instructed his reapers to leave large portions of wheat "accidentally on purpose" for the gleaning women to collect. The story ends like a romantic novel: Boaz marries Ruth, and they become ancestors of our Lord Jesus, who was born in Bethlehem.

How does all this relate to the Blessed Eucharist, in thanksgiving for which we are gathered here today? The clue to the link is the last line of today's Gospel, where we see Jesus' disciples gathering up the fragments of the bread, multiplied by Jesus in a miracle—looking forward to the Blessed Eucharist.

Monsignor Ronald Knox, in one of his pastoral sermons, once suggested that in the fields of the Holy Eucharist, you and I are gleaners as Ruth and Naomi were. We are not like Boaz's reapers, collecting large bundles; those hired hands were more like the saints. Don't we admit that in the field of the Blessed Eucharist—considering the relatively poor preparation we so frequently make and the brief thanksgiving, filled with all kinds of distractions—we barely manage to collect a few crumbs of spiritual nourishment? Yet even in this small collection, don't we understand that God is somehow making things especially easy for us?

Remember that when Boaz recognized Ruth, he told his reapers to drop some of the handfuls they gathered to make it easy for Ruth and Naomi to glean. Doesn't Christ, the owner of the Eucharist field, do the same for us? How else is it that we frequently *do* find ourselves receiving Communion with special devotion and making a good thanksgiving, despite all our wayward thoughts, or the heat, or the humidity, or our alleged fatigue? And doesn't Jesus help us glean in the field of the Eucharist precisely because he recognizes us as his kinsmen (as Boaz recognized Ruth)?

At Mass, as we approach the moment of Communion, it would be well for us to put ourselves in the person of Ruth, walking Christ's fields, hoping to collect a few fragments left over from his harvest, yet knowing all the time that he in his love will leave us large portions "accidentally on purpose." The portions *are* there, left by him, to be gathered by us, as were the fragments left over in the multiplication of the loaves, in today's Gospel reading.

Our act of gathering, in love, leads toward Jesus' claiming us for his own—as Boaz claimed Ruth.

For a Eucharistic Holy Hour (B)

(Exodus 24:3-8; First Corinthians 10:16-17; Luke 24:13-35)

We—we, the community of the redeemed in Christ—both recognize and meet the living Lord in the Eucharist, and are there united to him, and in him, with all men: this magnificent theme resounds through the Bible passages we have just listened to.

St. Paul, in the second passage, reminds Christians that the one bread in which we all share makes us one body in the Lord. And the Gospel reveals that we know the Lord in the Eucharist, the "breaking of bread."

Sacred Scripture tells us that Christ's Precious Blood was poured forth for all men in an entirely new covenant, prefigured by the sprinkling of the whole people with sacrificial blood in an earlier covenant with God—the first Biblical text, from Exodus. In every Mass the celebrant expressly recalls that Christ's Blood was shed for all persons, that sins might be forgiven. So the Mass and the Eucharist have social, communal dimensions.

This is not to say that participating in Mass, and receiving Communion, are not intensely personal acts. No; Mass and Communion *are* intensely personal. The effects of the Mass and Communion in my life—your life—depend upon the measure of our eucharistic union with Christ. Which means that the meaning of Mass and Communion are measured in our lives according to the faith and love in our hearts when we participate in Mass, and receive Communion.

The deeper our faith and love may be, the more perfect is our union with Christ. This, incidentally, answers a question which almost every adult Catholic asks himself at least by age 30: How can one go to Communion often—monthly, or even weekly—and not make substantial progress in Christian life? The Communions received—monthly or weekly for 10 or 20 years perhaps—are valid, certainly. These Communions were received in the state of grace. So that they were *worthy* in this sense. *But* these Communions—the Masses—failed to help one advance in discipleship precisely because better dispositions of faith and love were wanting. We must remind ourselves: the least distraction from faith in what we are doing at Mass, the least coolness entertained toward neighbor, can constitute major obstacles to the union which Christ wishes to have with us.

Again, attending Mass and receiving Communion are intensely personal encounters.

At the same time, however, the Mass and Communion are *social*, communal experiences. We attend Mass, we receive Communion, as individuals, yes; but *as individuals who go to make up the redeemed community of Christ*. There is no such thing as a private Mass. (Occasionally the phrase is used, but the Church discourages its use). Even when a priest offers the Eucharist alone, with but a server, he offers it in union with all Christians everywhere.

After all, isn't the Mass described not only as a memorial sacrifice, but also as a *banquet*? Does one attend a banquet all alone? Banquets presume a gathering. Christ instituted the Eucharist in the context of the Jewish Passover Banquet.

Or take the traditional verb for the Mass, "celebrate:" Does one celebrate all alone—without even mental reference to others? Of course not. Mass is celebrated; other people, therefore, are presumed; a communal action is implied.

One of the reasons for the Communion hymn and the Communion procession is the social aspect of the Eucharist. One doesn't process all alone; one *joins with others*. Thus we go to Communion in a group or groups, either to the Communion rail or to Communion stations. Hymn-singing at Communion is frequently used for the same reason that people join together in song while on a bus trip—to express unity.

Unity means of course that the people assembled sincerely care for one another, as Christ cared for all. It implies a commitment to suffering service in favor of neighbor, as Christ the Suffering Servant, humbled himself for us, even to the cross of Golgotha.

For a Eucharistic Holy Hour (C)

(First Corinthians 11:23-29; John 6:52-58)

Today's beautiful Bible texts focus on the doctrine of the Real Presence; namely, that in the Eucharist Jesus our Lord is really and truly present.

The doctrine of the Real Presence is a doctrine of faith. This means that we do not look to science, or even to philosophy, to ''prove'' it. No human science or discipline is competent here. We know about the Eucharist—that Jesus is really present in the Eucharist—because of God's word. The Bible and the Eucharist are inseparable.

What, specifically, is God's word in this area? How does the Church read the Bible here? Read the Last Supper accounts in the first three Gospels, or in St. Paul to the Corinthians (today's first Bible lesson). Jesus, we are told, offered his own Body and Blood for us. He did not say, ''This is a sign of my body,'' or ''This symbolizes my body.'' His words are direct and clear: ''This *is* my body.''

In fact, some time before the Last Supper, when Jesus first promised us the Eucharist, he sadly witnessed many of his disciples walking away precisely because he insisted on describing himself *as the bread of life*—not (again) as a *symbol* of the bread of life. Some of his followers vocally complained; they found his words too literal. ''This is intolerable language,'' they said. ''How could anyone accept it?''

The Gospel we have just read recalls these complaints. New words are invented, new phrases formulated, new theories put together, to ''explain away'' the clear revelation of the Bible: namely, that the Eucharist is not merely a sign, but a sign that is a reality. The Eucharist is real food; real drink; again, recall the Gospel, John 6.

St. Paul, in our first lesson today, flatly stated that the Eucharist is the

Body and Blood of the Lord so much so that to receive it unworthily—in the state of serious sin—is to sin against the very body of Jesus (11:26, 27).

In the Eucharist, we experience a certain epiphany of God: the risen Lord Jesus really present in our midst. We use the word Real Presence—a medieval phrase—not in the sense that Christ isn't really present in the other sacraments, or in the Church, or in the Christian assembly, or in the Bible—but to emphasize that, in the Eucharist, Christ is personally, uniquely, supremely, sacramentally present.

St. Thomas Aquinas, one of the greatest minds the Church has ever produced, and who at death acknowledged Christ in the Eucharist as central to all his monumental theological writings, summarized our faith in the Real Presence in one of his immortal hymns, the *Adoro te devote*. These words, from the opening verses, are to be taken literally:

> O Godhead hid, devoutly I adore Thee,
> Who truly art within the forms before me;
> To Thee my heart I bow with bended knee,
> As failing quite in contemplating Thee.
> Sight, touch, and taste in Thee are each deceived;
> The ear alone most safely is believed:
> I believe all the Son of God has spoken,
> Than Truth's own word there is no truer token . . .
> (translation by E. Caswell; from *The Raccolta*, New York: Benziger, 1943)

For A Communion Breakfast (Supper)

Diogenes the Cynic (d. 323 B.C.)—the same Greek who once walked around Athens with a lantern searching for an honest man—onced asked to be buried upside down. Why? "Because," he said, "in a little while everything will be turned upside down."

The world has literally turned upside down many times since, and today it is spinning again, spinning in confusion, a confusion so intense that even otherwise stable people are in danger of losing their balance.

Not that all this has not happened before. Confusion and chaos were widespread after the Great Persecutions, for example, beginning in the fourth century. And in the late Middle Ages the situation was so critical that St. Thomas Aquinas, the Church's supreme theologian, prayed, when he began teaching and writing: "Lord, save me, for truths are disappearing from amongst the children of men."

We could all pray the same prayer today. Prayer is really an affirmation of faith. Faith is the means by which we maintain stability in changing times, balance in the midst of confusion. There are certain truths we hold in faith, and we know for certain that these truths are enduring, so enduring that we can literally stake our lives on them.

My first message at this Communion Breakfast (Supper) then is a call to faith. Today especially, we must all be persons (men, women) of faith, all committed unreservedly to the truth which faith alone provides.

Faith in the living Lord Jesus gives meaning to every honest corner or fact of our earthly pilgrimage; there is nothing worth talking about that cannot be discussed in the context of faith.

Moreover, faith is not a leap in the dark, but progress from dark or grey to light. Faith frees us from pressure put on us by the world as a whole to vacillate about basic truth, to "waffle," as they say. Waffling is reflected in current phrases like, "But that's your view." It's often said, for example, in response to statements like, "Direct abortion is evil," or "Marriage is a sacred institution meant as a lifetime commitment."

Why waffle? Why be afraid, or hesitate, to take a stand? Why not stand up against the tide of confusion and absurdity of our age?

Why should a Christian prefer uncertainty about areas in which he or she, of all men, can have certitude?

A Christian knows that there is a God, who became incarnate in Jesus Christ. About this he (she) can be sure.

A Christian knows that, beyond any question, Jesus is the way, the truth, and the life; that, in other words, to live humanly and meaningfully, one must live as a disciple of Jesus, who will judge each one of us at death.

Jesus' way is clearly set forth in his word: in the Bible as read by, and within, Jesus' Church. Jesus' way is a way of humble suffering service for others in his name; a way of peacemaking, of purity of heart and integrity and justice and mercy; of faith, hope, and love. It is not a way of prejudice or pride or greed or adultery or fornication or abortion or murder or sexual license or dissension or rash judgment or pessimism or dishonesty or selfishness. About all this, we have certainty.

What the Bible tells us about the sanctity of marriage, about the need for prayer, about the essence of personal fulfillment, about the shallowness of a godless existence: all these can and must be received with certainty, with absolute, unreserved certainty.

Not only must we be persons of faith; further, our faith must be confident. This is the second message I should like to convey this morning (evening). Lack of confidence, someone has observed, can be just as destructive to a society as bombs can be.

As believers in the midst of confusion, our faith must be confident, and must *inspire* confidence—the kind of confidence that is nourished and confirmed supremely in the Eucharist, for which we have all assembled here today.

PART III

SPECIAL DEVOTIONS

For a Bible Vigil

Isaiah 55:11; Hebrews 4:12-13; Choice of Gospel

"God's word," the Epistle to the Hebrews reminds us "is living and effective, sharper than any two-edged sword" (4:12).

This means that the Bible, together with the preached Word, is dynamic, efficacious of faith, and extremely keen.

How unsophisticated we are who think that ultimate wisdom can more readily, or more thoroughly, be discovered elsewhere: in psychology and sociology, for instance, for all their merits.

How unsophisticated too are those who would substitute the word of God—the Bible and the proclaimed Gospel—with discussion periods, films and slides, or even sensitivity sessions.

It is our faith that nothing can take the place of Scripture or the preached Gospel; nothing. Again, it is dynamic, efficacious of faith and keen.

It is dynamic. The word of God is mysteriously alive. It can never be read twice under the same circumstances. Each and every time it is heard, proclaimed, or studied, an entirely new situation becomes present to the listener or reader.

In a sense this is true of great human literature. Dante's *Divine Comedy* is read differently at age 40, say, than it was at age 20: so too, are the great novels of Tolstoy and Dostoevsky; or the reflections of Pascal. But in such instances the new situation is but a unilateral creation; every fresh approach to works of art depends on the subjective dispositions of the reader.

This is not true of the word of God. Each and every time it is encountered, an entirely new opportunity for faith and grace—what the New Testament calls a *kairos*—occurs; God presents himself to us anew.

Kairos, a Greek derivative, signifies the critical moment; the *Now*, as we say. It focuses on this particular hour of grace and trial granted us by God. (The ancient Greeks even had a god named *Kairos*, to whom they prayed, one supposes, for the light and courage to seize each opportunity as it presented itself).

The word of God is, secondly, productive of God-life. To the well-disposed it can effect and nourish faith in the heart of anyone who opens his or her heart to listen. As our First Reading from Isaiah reveals, God's word comes as the rain: "It shall not return to me void, but shall do my will, achieving the end for which I sent it" (55:11).

Finally, the word of God is keen—sharper than a two-edged sword. It cuts at the very heart, doesn't it, to hear that our somewhat qualified commitment to Christianity is not commitment enough? Jesus' "Come, follow me," is a startling summons to total dedication. Every paragraph of the Bible sounds a similar challenge, entails a similar "moment of truth."

The sanctity and the power of the Bible were repeatedly emphasized by the Fathers of Vatican Council II. One of the most eloquent witnesses in this regard appears in the Dogmatic constitution on Divine Revelation, Section 21:

"The Church has always venerated the divine Scripture just as she venerates the body of the Lord, since from the table of both the word of God and of the body of Christ she unceasingly receives and offers to the faithful the bread of life, especially in the sacred liturgy. She has always regarded the Scriptures together with sacred tradition as the supreme rule of faith, and will ever do so. For, inspired by God and committed once and for all to writing, they impart the word of God himself without change, and make the voice of the Holy Spirit resound in the words of the prophets and apostles."

As a result of today's Bible vigil, we should resolve to read (or continue the practice of reading) the Bible more often, perhaps at least ten minutes daily. We must become convinced that *this is our book of wisdom*, that it gives us the enlightenment to go forward in Christian witness and that it provides us with the power of a two-edged sword against the evils of the time.

For a Sacred Heart Devotion
(First Friday)

Devotion to the Sacred Heart of Jesus should not be imagined as a sentimental luxury for religious introverts, or dismissed as an old-fashioned relic of yesterday's piety.

Besides, as theologian Karl Rahner asks, "What is old-fashioned? What is modern? The really modern Christian is not the man who makes a point of non-conformity to a certain past and conforms to a today that only shallow minds take for the future . . . No, the rare, resolute people who find the things of tomorrow in those of yesterday are the ones to tell us what today really is." In the Sacred Heart devotion "we adore the heart that plunged, oblivious of self, into the deadly solitude of our guilt and the frightful incomprehensibility of God, abandoning itself to the dull routine of everyday, the irksome tasks of routine service" (*Servants of the Lord*: Sheed and Ward, 1967).

The real Sacred Heart devotion does not simply constitute a statue of Jesus pointing to his wounded heart; it does not constitute "making the nine first Fridays of the month;" it does not constitute memorizing certain promises made in private revelations.

What devotion to the Sacred Heart does mean is that the humanity of Jesus, through which the Son of God Incarnate suffered and died for love of us, constitutes the fulfillment of Jacob's Ladder reaching from earth to heaven (Gn 28:12 and Jn 1:51).

In honoring the Sacred Heart, therefore, we affirm that there is nothing at all sacred, there is nothing at all good (not an atom in the whole of creation), which does not presuppose, as instrumental cause, some act of the humanity assumed by the Son of God-made-man, Jesus. There is no divine grace that does not entail an act of Jesus' knowledge of us, and his love for us. This doctrine provides the most solid foundation possible for the Sacred Heart devotion.

This is not to deny that a kind of crisis surrounds the state of the devotion today. But the crisis is really one of who and how many Catholics will have the courage to try to grasp the meaning of the Sacred Heart in accordance with its biblical significance, sans the accidental, and, sometimes, questionable features which have been attached to it by popular piety and usage.

Again, the center of the dovotion is not—never has been—the so-called "nine first Fridays." The truth is that the first Friday devotion—participating in the Eucharist on the first Friday of the month, or for nine First Fridays in succession—is only a means (one highly approved by the Church, of course) of practising the devotion. The center is that the sacred humanity of Jesus is the only place where God has made physical contact with this world. And it is a contact overflowing with love, symbolized by Jesus' pierced heart (Jn 19:32).

When we look upon the pierced heart of Christ our Savior, then, we are confronted with an awesome sign as to how God loves us; namely God's becoming incarnate so that he might suffer and die to redeem us and ensure our being with him forever. So that there is nothing piously sentimental about the real Sacred Heart devotion.

Rather, (to quote Rahner again) "it is terrible—terrible in its dark death-throes; terrible in the incomprehensible mystery of the love whereby God exposes himself to his creatures, their guilt and futility, terrible in the absolute claim it lays on us, sweeping us away into its destiny; terrible in the confidence with which it reaches out to our appalling unreliability" (*Ibid.*)

Viewed in this sense, devotion to the Sacred Heart is not optional (as, for example, devotion to the Infant Jesus of Prague is), but goes to the very essence of our relationship with the living Lord. Whenever we contemplate Christ in his pierced heart we can hardly ignore the over-whelming love he has for us, despite our sinfulness. If we only allow the Spirit to pray within us, we shall find ourselves calling upon the Lord in our own heart, experiencing within ourselves the wounds which our dear Savior accepted that we might live in God's grace.

By its very nature true devotion to the Sacred Heart of Jesus demands an intense *personal* awareness, so as to permit love for love rendered. Assisting at Mass on the first Friday of the month is a potent means toward arriving at such an awareness.

For the Way of the Cross

The Way of the Cross, for which we are assembled, ranks alongside the Rosary of the Blessed Virgin Mary as among the Church's best loved and most highly indulgenced devotions.

Also known as the Stations of the Cross ("Stations" derives from the Latin word for "stops along the way"), this devotion originated in and just outside Jerusalem, where our divine Lord carried the cross, died, was buried, and rose from the dead. St. Jerome (d. 420) testified to it in his time.

It is argued by some historians that the first Way of the Cross *outside* the Holy Land appeared during the fifth century, in the Church of San Stefano, in Bologna. Only five "stations" or "stops" were assigned there, however.

The 14 Stations we know today evidently date from around the 16th century; the number and structure of the present devotion were determined by Pope Clement XII in 1731.

The popularity of the Way of the Cross throughout the world is due largely to the efforts of the Franciscans, who assumed supervision of the holy places of Jerusalem in 1342. Viewing it their privilege to promulgate this devotion, they preached it in their monasteries, churches and shrines, from where it spread to parish churches, such as our parish church.

Of the 14 stations we know, a few are not found in the Bible. The sixth Station, *Veronica Wipes the Face of Jesus*, is the best known example. The three falls of Jesus beneath the Cross constitute others. These "stations" have come down to us by means of tradition.

Making the Way of the Cross simply requires meditation on the Passion and death of Christ, plus corporal movement from one station to another (unless the devotion is made with a group, in which case it is sufficient that the leader move from station to station).

No specific prayers are necessary. Again, all that is needed is that one reflect prayerfully—experience loving thought—on the Passion and death of the Lord.

Sometimes, especially in the Way of the Cross made publicly, vocal prayers (e.g., Paters, Aves) and special readings are used.

The stations themselves are not the pictures or plaques depicting Jesus' Passion and death but rather the 14 crosses. The scenes of Christ beneath or over the blessed crosses are only aids to meditation.

A plenary indulgence may be gained for making the Way of the Cross. Those who are impeded—e.g., the seriously ill who cannot get to church—can acquire the same indulgence by spending at least a half hour in pious reading and meditation on the Passion and death of our Lord (*Enchiridion of Indulgences*, 1968).

The Way of the Cross ends with Jesus' burial—and his Resurrection. When one stands before the 14th Station, one should not forget that the same tomb in which Christ was buried, became the place of his Resurrection on Easter Sunday. As the Gospels conclude the story of Jesus' death with his rising, so should we.

Thus, one method of concluding the Way of the Cross is by recalling the faith-acclamation we say at Mass: ''Christ has died, Christ is risen, Christ will come again.''

As we begin this Way of the Cross today, we should be intensely aware of what we are doing—*being privileged* to do. Literally, we are relocating ourselves in spirit to the *Via Dolorosa* and Calvary, in order to follow our Lord and Savior Jesus Christ in his sacrificial pilgrimage to the cross for our sake. May Mary the mother of the Lord help us enter into this pilgrimage of faith, hope and love—a Way for which we are not worthy.

For a Marian Devotion

Devotion to Mary the Mother of the Lord necessarily orients toward Jesus. In the language of theology, all Marian devotion must be Christocentric.

We know this principle from the Bible.

Never once in the New Testament is Mary mentioned without reference to her divine Son, at least implicitly.

At the Annunciation, our Lady was asked to be *Jesus' mother.* "Listen! You are to conceive and bear a son, and you must name him Jesus" (Lk 1:31).

In Matthew's genealogy, Mary's name is immediately followed by a specific *reference to Jesus.* . . . "And Jacob was the father of Joseph the husband of Mary; of her was born Jesus who is called Christ" (Mt 1:16).

The Visitation account recalls the sanctifying power of the Word made flesh, *Jesus, within Mary's womb.* "Of all women you are the most blessed, and blessed is the fruit of your womb. Why should I be honored with a visit from the mother of my Lord?" (Lk 1:42).

St. Luke's beautiful Nativity narrative focuses not on Mary, but on *Jesus' birth* in the manger. ". . . She gave birth to a son, her first-born. She wrapped him in swaddling clothes, and laid him in a manger . . . " (Lk 2:7).

Jesus' presentation in the Temple is emphasized in Luke's Purification scene. "(Simeon) took Jesus into his arms and blessed God . . . You see this child: he is destined for the fall and rising of many in Israel . . . " (Lk 2:28, 34).

Mary's anxiety over her son's being lost in the Temple is told from the viewpoint of *Jesus' vocation.* "Were you looking for me? Did you not know that I must be busy with my Father's affairs?" (Lk 2:49).

Even the Gospel's few lines concerning Mary's home life at Nazareth point to the *mystery of Jesus*. "His mother stored up all these things in her heart" (Lk 2:52).

When Mary is mentioned in the text about the wedding in Cana of Galilee *she turns to Jesus*. "They have no wine . . . Do whatever he tells you" (Jn 2:4, 5).

When our Lady's visit to Capernaum is recorded, she is depicted *with Jesus*. " . . . He went down to Capernaum with his mother . . . " (Jn 2:12).

As Matthew interrupts his narrative to refer to our Lady during Jesus' public ministry, he recalls *an incident directly pertaining to Christ*. "He was still speaking to the crowds when his mother and brothers appeared . . . " (Mt 12:46).

And the final glimpse we have of Mary in the Gospels until the Resurrection is as the Madonna standing *beneath the Cross of Jesus*. "Near the cross of Jesus stood his mother . . . " (Jn 19:25).

Even after the first Easter, the reference to Mary in the Acts of the Apostles identifies her as *"the mother of Jesus"* (Ac 1:14).

How Marian devotion must be essentially Christocentric can be clearly seen in the Church's principal nonliturgical Marian prayer, the Rosary. If one really thinks carefully about it, he sooner or later must come to the conclusion that the Rosary is addressed directly not to the Virgin but to Christ. It is a series of meditations, accompanied by a series of vocal prayers, on the Christ-event; Mary is always there, but in the background.

For a Rosary Devotion

We are gathered today not only to pray, but also to reflect upon, one of the Church's most beloved and highly indulgenced devotions, the Rosary of the Blessed Virgin Mary.

How shall we approach our reflection? By accenting the power of the Rosary—the mysterious event of Lepanto, for example, of which G.K. Chesterton sang in one of the most impressive instances of lyric poetry in the English language? Or shall we rehearse some of the countless wonders of grace experienced by those who have been devoted to the Rosary: wonders symbolized in the simple Rosary beads found among the archaeological diggings of the 17th century Indian villages in upper New York State, where St. Isaac Jogues and the North American Martyrs first brought the banner of Christ to our nation?

On the other hand, wouldn't it be more useful to reflect on the power of the Rosary *for us*? Not on what the Rosary has achieved in human history, but what it can achieve *here and now*, in our times, in this hour of history? And what it can contribute to our future self-making?

What can the Rosary do for us? Now?

First, because the Rosary is a prayer—a meditation accompanied by Our Fathers and Hail Marys—it can be both a reminder and an affirmation of Transcendence.

This is crucial today since we live in an environment of secularism. Secularism alleges, simply, that everything real can be explained, adequately if not wholly, on the horizontal level. The vertical plane can't even be discussed; there is neither any serious attempt to reject God nor to admit his possibility; God simply isn't talked about, and reality is "reduced" to the horizontal plane.

Prayer is an unequivocal affirmation of Transcendence, of a vertical plane, just as real as the horizontal plane. The moment a man sincerely begins a prayer—like the Rosary—he in effect repudiates the secularist premise in which our late-twentieth century technological world is immersed.

Secondly, the power of the Rosary for us is, in a sense, the power of the Bible, God's sustaining word. Pope John XXIII once described the Rosary in terms of the Bible. The Rosary is really a kind of Bible devotion. Thirteen of the 15 mysteries are explicitly drawn from the Gospels; the remaining two (the Assumption and Glorification of our Lady) are implicitly Scriptural. In fact, the Rosary constitutes a mental pilgrimage through the pages of the New Testament.

The more one meditates on the mysteries, the more one is drawn to the events detailed in the pertinent Bible texts; and the more one studies the pertinent Bible texts, the more profoundly he or she can experience the depths of the Rosary.

Who can say the Rosary—sincerely, I mean—and not desire to go back to the Bible again and again, to learn more and more about salvation history, and not desire to read the Bible daily and to be present frequently at Mass, where the treasures of the Bible are opened up and preached on?

There is more. When we say the Rosary, our Lady is mysteriously in our midst and prays with us—as surely she was praying with the first Christian community in the Upper Room that historic Pentecost week when the Paraclete descended and besouled the Church.

When Mary prays with us, she strengthens us in two ways: (1) she keeps us oriented toward Jesus; and (2) she sustains us in faith.

Despite all her privileges—her being called to be Mother of the Lord, her immaculate conception—Mary had to walk the same path which every disciple of Jesus must walk: the path of faith.

Because Mary kept faith she is the actualization of the perfect Christian: one who remains completely open in absolute, unreserved, hopeful, loving faith. And she is also the "sign" of the perfect Christian, the model to be followed.

As the person of faith par excellence, Mary points to Jesus—always. The Rosary itself is not addressed directly to Mary, but to Jesus.

At a Wake Service

We are gathered at a Wake Service following the death of a loved one. "Wake" derives from a medieval English word meaning "vigil" or "watch." As Christians we view the wake primarily as a prayer vigil. We are here chiefly to pray for the deceased and to reflect prayerfully on God's word regarding death and bereavement. Even our words of sympathy to the family and relatives of the deceased on this occasion are words reflecting prayer.

Prayer is an expression of faith. Faith is at the heart of our Christian response to death. It is in faith that we, the bereaved, come to realize that while death is always shocking and traumatic, it is nonetheless a natural phenomenon which we *can deal with* through God's word and grace. In faith we learn that while death occasions sadness, and consequently, mourning, it is not simply a meaningless occurrence, but rather a mystery essentially defined in terms of an eternal homecoming.

In faith, moreover, we come to know that in Jesus' Resurrection all who believe in him are called to rise in the flesh to everlasting life; that our prayers here and now can assist those who have gone before us in Christ; that the living Lord Jesus supports us who are left behind in the death of a loved one: comforts us in our grief, strengthens us in our depression and feelings of isolation, helps us redefine our roles, and encourages us to get on with living as best we can with his help.

Thus, one of the opening greetings of this Vigil Service or Wake begins with Jesus' words recorded in Matthew 11:28:

> Come to me, all who are weary and find life
> burdensome, and I will refresh you.

Faith of course pertains to the whole person. Hence it is no surprise to us, as Christians, to realize that this Prayer Vigil or Wake can also help us psychologically as well as spiritually. For one thing, this service can serve as a countermeasure against the natural temptation to withdraw from reality—a temptation especially current in today's "denial of death" climate. To put it another way, wakes can help facilitate the very human grieving process.

Grief, it should be emphasized, is a perfectly normal human reaction; Jesus, recall, wept at Lazarus' grave. Dr. Francis J. Braceland, in *Modern Psychiatry, A Handbook for Believers*, quotes from Leigh Hunt:

> "It is only for sophists to contend that we, whose eyes contain the fountains of tears, need never give way to them. It would be unwise not to do so on some occasions. Sorrow unlocks them in her balmy moods. The first bursts may be bitter and overwhelming, but the soil on which they pour would be worse without them."

The grieving process, psychologists suggest, can last at least six months, sometimes longer, in perfectly normal situations. And it can be described as occurring in various stages, including feelings of loneliness, anxiety, panic, guilt and inertia; attendant physical symptoms are also part of the general process. The wake can help the bereaved to face, and begin to experience this normal process of grieving.

Again, though, the key to our being here is faith. It is faith which, more than anything else, helps us at this moment of trial. Our prayers on this occasion express this faith. At the same time they affirm it.

PART IV

JUBILEES AND ANNIVERSARIES

For a Wedding Anniversary

Today, on the occasion of this twenty-fifth (fiftieth) anniversary of a Christian marriage, we congratulate with a couple, N and N, who so faithfully kept their vows of love, once made in and with the living Lord Jesus. And we pray that Christ will continue to bless and glorify their marriage.

The occasion also prompts reflection on what we in faith describe as the permanence of Christian marriage. For us, marriage is by its nature permanent. This is expressed in the "consent" given by the bride and groom on their wedding day, when each says (or ratifies) the phrase, "I will love you and honor you all the days of my life." An alternate form is the familiar "until death do us part."

How can we be so certain—absolutely certain—that marriage is permanent, and that it will always remain permanent? How is it that we can summarily reject theories—propagated by some psychologists or sociologists or the media—that marriage as we know it may be a thing of the past, and that marriage needn't entail a permanent commitment?

The answer is that we know because we have a Revelation. God's word, which transcends essentially the feeble efforts of mortals to perfectly understand, tells us unequivocally that when a man and a woman exchange marital vows in Christ they enter into an enduring, holy union that cannot be broken save by the death of a spouse.

God's word tells us this; the Bible as read within the Church makes this clear. Greater certainty is not possible than that derived from Truth itself. Read Mark 10:6-9 for example; or Matthew 9:14. Or read Ephesians 5:32.

The permanence of matrimony is crucial for Christians. One reason is the very dignity of the human person (a reason that should be especially meaningful today, with all the emphasis on "being a person"). As Pope Pius XII explained in an address to newlyweds on April 29, 1942:

> Married cohabitation is a divine institution rooted in human nature as a union of two beings made to the image and likeness of God, who calls them to continue his work in the preservation and propagation of mankind. There is rooted and living in the consciousness of both husband and wife a desire to belong totally one to the other, to remain faithful to each other in all the changes and chances of life, in the days of happiness and sadness, in health and sickness, in their first years together as in their later years, without limit or conditions, until God wishes to call them to eternity. In this consciousness, in these intentions, human dignity is exalted . . . When this is not verified, common life runs the risk of sliding into the pit of selfish desire, which seeks nothing but its own satisfaction and thinks not of the personal dignity and honor of the partner.

The permanence of Christian marriage is mysteriously linked with the sanctity of Christian marriage. For a believer, marriage not only represents Christ's union with his Church, but as a sacrament establishes so intimate a supernatural bond that the spouses are assumed into the mystery of Redemption in a unique and precise manner.

Another way to express this theology is to say that Christian marriage entails not only a sacred contract between a man and a woman, but also a covenant with the living Lord Jesus, who irrevocably pledges his love and guidance to the couple who are made one in him.

The saying, "it takes three to get married," is no empty phrase. Committed, loving fidelity to this doctrine is what we are witnessing at this holy anniversary.

For the Jubilee of a Woman Religious

We are met today for a Eucharist marking an especially memorable occasion for one of the Sisters (Nuns), for her relatives and friends, and for this community: the silver (golden) jubilee of Sister N.

This event invites us not only to joyful celebration, but also to prayerful review. Surely one of the dimensions of a jubilee in vowed commitment is reflection on the meaning of religious dedication.

One way of viewing the evangelical vows is with respect to the whole context of Christian living, a context suggested by the Beatitudes (today's Gospel), that beautiful litany of ''Blesseds'' which epitomizes the core and the height of discipleship in Christ.

If we should search the New Testament Scriptures for an adequate description of a Christian lifestyle, we would eventually settle on three key terms: fellowship, service and witness. Or, to put this another way, the Christian's outlook on the world rests upon the tripod of community, suffering service and witness.

Is not this what vowed religious commitment in poverty, chastity and obedience is meant to serve and to ensure in an extraordinary degree? Further, is it not true that religious commitment helps focus the mysteries of community, suffering service and witness?

Take the first aspect of genuine evangelical style: fellowship. Isn't a religious society defined in terms of community? Interpersonal inspiring, sharing, concern, healing, supporting, caring, all against the backdrop of a common purpose?

Secondly, take service. Surely this too is the obligation of everyone baptized in Christ; namely, to follow faithfully in the footsteps of the Suffering Servant of Yahweh prophesied long ago by Isaiah. Vowed service both formalizes and intensifies fulfillment of this fundamental

Christian imperative. It impels one when fatigue or age or health tempts one to slow down; it keeps reminding one that Jesus' cross was heavier than the disciples'; it provides new strength and determination when one's total efforts seem at times so insignificant or ineffectual when measured against the work that must be done, or the work that others have already done.

Lastly, consider witness, the third key aspect of the Church's style, and, as such, incumbent on all who call upon the name of Jesus. "Witness" derives from the Greek for "martyrdom." What more dramatic sign of witness is there than taking the evangelical vows? Isn't poverty a sign to the effect that one accepts, with her whole heart, the central message of Jesus' parable of the Lilies of the Field? Isn't vowed obedience an especially dramatic sign of the glad acceptance of the concrete circumstances of community life with its grey areas and obscurities?

And what of chastity? Is there a more sacrificial sign of loving dedication? By it, religious witness to that wondrous marriage between Christ and the Church, his spouse: a union founded by God and which will be fully manifested in the world to come.

The members of each community, the Fathers of Vatican II affirm, "have handed over their entire lives to God's service in an act of special consecration which is deeply rooted in their baptismal consecration and which provides a greater manifestation of it" (*Decree on the Appropriate Renewal of the Religious Life*, Sec. 5).

This is what Sister N. has lived valiantly. She has intensified her baptismal commitment to Christian fellowship, suffering service, and Gospel witness by virtue of the vows she took 25 (50) years ago in this congregation, which is but the Church in miniature. Today we thank her for her fidelity to these vows—those of us who have been graced by her presence. We share in her joy. We pray for her especially at this hour. And we wish her Godspeed in the years to come.

PART V

ECUMENISM AND INTERFAITH

For the Ecumenical Movement (General)

Ecumenism has to do with the quest for Christian unity. As such it can be approached from several angles.

One is historical. There are those who feel that a useful approach is to rehearse, insofar as is possible, the incidents and circumstances which have resulted in today's fragmented Christianity. In this view ecumenism is largely like a movie reel of Christian history run backwards until it runs off the reel. History, however, is complex and difficult.

Another dimension of the quest is of course theological. But theology, like history, is also complex and difficult. Besides, as Cardinal John Heenan of England once observed: ". . . It is not for theologians to devise formulae which will produce external unity or compose a vague creed to which all Christians could subscribe only by use of mental reservations" (The London *Tablet*, January 24, 1970).

A third approach toward ecumenism is that which we are accenting here today: a common testifying, by prayer, to faith in the living Lord Jesus, who calls us to his embrace now and at the Omega Point of our own historicity; and to a bond of love which draws us together in the name of the Lord whom we call upon.

It is this bond of love which, in the ultimate analysis, will eventually bring us all together. There is no surer way of moving toward union than by our practising the law of fraternal charity. Which is to say that we must be persons for others. Our characteristic stance in the world must be one not of co-existence, but of pro-existence—to borrow a phrase once used by Dr. David H.C. Read of New York City's Madison Avenue Presbyterian Church.

Pro-existence means, first and foremost, that the Christian must be concerned about others, sympathetic to their problems and needs, and attuned to their anxieties. Like Jesus, the Suffering Servant of Yahweh par excellence prophesied long ago by Isaiah, the Christian must reach out in service to his neighbors.

The Church, Cardinal Richard Cushing argued in a pastoral letter issued in Advent of 1967, cannot share Jesus' exaltation until "she has followed with him in the path of humiliation and suffering service." Hence the disciple must be outgoing, must be a "sacrament" for others; must involve himself in the healing mission of Christ by sharing with others a passion for justice, sensitivity and compassion in the face of the poor and the downtrodden; must, in a word, be (as Dietrich Bonhoeffer said) a person "for others." Such suffering service ensures our deepest longings to be united in Christ.

Today we could make a fresh commitment to "pro-existence," living for others for God's sake; being persons for others, for love of Jesus; entering into suffering service in the footsteps of the Master.

This is true ecumenism on the grassroots level. And it is a level on which we can all meet and work and agonize, *and rejoice*.

Rejoice, I say, because Christ our Savior himself told us that in relating to others for his sake, we discover him (Mt 25:31-46). And *he*—the living Lord Jesus—is the goal of all our ecumenical gatherings and journeyings. What we are *ultimately* striving for is not a consensus statement, or collaboration in certain practices, or even a common creed in the abstract, but rather the person of the risen Savior, who draws us toward him even now with his merciful love, and guides us to his embrace so that we may all be one in him, as he is one with the Father in the unity of the Holy Spirit.

Applying the phrase St. Augustine used so many centuries ago to our purpose here, we can all say, in faith: "It is *you*, O Lord, whom we seek in this ecumenical meeting."

For the Ecumenical Movement (Ministers)
(A Sermon Directed to Priests and Ministers
Gathered For Ecumenical Prayer and Reflection)

Ministers of the Gospel, we are met here today for ecumenical prayer and reflection.

One point to ponder is that we have all much work to do if Jesus' prayer for unity is to be realized in the foreseeable future (Jn 17:20, 21). And at the head of the agenda is our witnessing to the reality of Christ, and to the validity of his word, in a world whose mind set is largely secularist.

Malcolm Muggeridge, in *Jesus Rediscovered*, writes of "a very large number of letters" he has received throughout life attesting to "the extraordinary spiritual hunger which prevails today among all classes and conditions of people." It is a hunger, he notes, which is not assuaged by such things as legalized abortion, or solaced by contraception, or relieved by majority rule. No; the only means of satisfying it, he writes, "remains that bread of life which Jesus offered, with the promise that those who ate of it would never hunger again."

Witnessing to this wisdom is our common responsibility, and we cannot avoid it. God's word is ultimate wisdom. God exists; he is Tripersonal; he rewards the virtuous and punishes evildoers; he created man to know, love, and serve him in this world, and be happy with him forever in the next; he touched this world in the Sacred Humanity of his only Son, Jesus of Nazareth, who suffered, died, and rose from the grave that he might live with us; these are key truths toward which all ecumenism necessarily orients.

Muggeridge has something specifically to say to ministers (and spokespersons) for Christianity who have allowed themselves to forget the one Bread that can fulfill our deepest hunger and instead have begun to substitute human talk for God talk, secularist humanism for Biblical truth. His assessment is that such individuals simply have lost faith.

Having been misled into dismissing the Transcendental notion (and all that it encompasses) by the confused and wayward prophets of secularism, he argues, these once committed men (and women) desperately need something to say in order to retain their pulpits or academic chairs. And in their straits they have largely turned to the fallacious ideology that man can satisfy his ultimate aspirations in worldly terms. In effect, they have thereby translated revealed doctrines regarding human fulfilment (e.g., the Kingdom of God, the final judgments, the Beatific Vision, heaven and hell) into terms of a merely secularist theory.

The message here, obviously, is that we must be persons of faith. Without faith we have no *raison d'etre*. This gathering can be an occasion for each one of us to renew his (or her) faith commitment. Concretely, in our meditation we could reaffirm our dedication to the Bible as read within the Church as our ultimate font of wisdom; we could restate our acceptance of the reality of God's intervention in our world: the great mysteries of the Incarnation, Redemption, Resurrection. We could prayerfully renew our belief in the truth that Jesus *lives, intervenes* in our lives, and *awaits* us now at Point Omega.

Lord, Jesus Christ, help us be enlightened, courageous heralds of the holy ecumenical movement, especially through a solid, brilliant unreserved, enthusiastic, and *joyous* faith. Help us realize that we must not only be immersed in faith, but that our belief in you and your word will literally radiate from us.

Confirm us in our resolve and help this resolution draw us all together toward the unity for which Jesus your Son, our Lord, prayed so earnestly the night before he died for us on Calvary's cross. We ask this through the same Christ our Lord. Amen.

For the Ecumenical Movement
(Eastern Orthodox)

Whenever we meet for dialogue, study, or prayer, we cannot avoid recollections of sad chapters of Church history concerning our two Churches: the Orthodox Churches of the Byzantine Tradition and the Roman Catholic Church.

The tragic schism, we recall, was consummated in 1054 when Michael Cerularius was Patriarch of Constantinople (Istanbul).

Factors which contributed to the rift were however discernible as early as the ninth century. One was the dispute between Photius, who became Patriarch of Constantinople in 858, and Pope Nicholas I (856-867). These factors, which are highly complex, were still at work when in 1054 mutual excommunication was decreed by Constantinople and Rome.

These censures were simultaneously removed by Rome and Constantinople on December 7, 1965. In a joint declaration issued by Pope Paul VI and Athenagoras I and his Holy Synod, it was agreed:

"Nothing can be done to take away these actual events of that particularly troubled period of history and make them to have never been. But nowadays, when they have been judged more calmly and fairly, it is important to recognize the excesses that marked them later led to consequences that, as far as we can judge, went far beyond the original intentions and expectations of their authors, who were directing the censures toward the individuals involved and not toward Churches. They did not intend to break ecclesiastical communion between the sees of Rome and Constantinople."

In this historic document, Pope Paul and Athenagoras formally regretted the unfortunate events of 1054, as well as all the consequences that contributed to an effective break in communion. At the same time, these two charismatic Churchmen, to whom we are so indebted, expressed the hope that the mutual lifting of the excommunications would be but a beginning of highly graced events, even ''an invitation to carry on, in a spirit of confidence, esteem and mutual charity, the dialogue that with God's help'' will bring Constantinople and Rome together again ''for the greater good of souls and the advancement of the Kingdom of God, in the full communion of faith, fraternal harmony and sacramental life that existed between them in the course of the first thousand years of the Church's life.''

From our side, Pope John Paul II is now pressing forward toward the day when union can be again achieved. (His first major move in this direction occurred in late November 1979, during his pilgrimage to Istanbul). Like Paul VI, the Holy Father is acting on the premise that ecumenical activity need not focus on a rerun of historical chapters. It is important to understand what happened in the past, and why. But the past is past; we live in the Now. The forces that were at work then, are no longer viable; ours is a new world, a new age, and a fresh opportunity. Knowing the past should help us avoid its mistakes. Knowing that we have a fresh chance to set things aright, should persuade us not to squander the opportunity.

In their search for keys to reunion, both Paul VI and John Paul II pilgrimaged to Ephesus, a place almost synonymous with Mary, the Mother of the Lord. Mary is one of the sure signposts that both our Traditions seek for, and confidently follow. Today, gathered in an ecumenical session in miniature, we could do no better than commend ourselves to her—*theotokos*—in a special way, in a special prayer, for special graces. We pray that she may help us be worthy of the privileged task which the Lord now entrusts to us. Together we can sing, from the hymn of the shepherds in the morning service of *Akathistos* Saturday:

> Joy to thee, Mother of the Lamb and the Shepherd.
> Joy to thee, Herder of spiritual sheep . . .
> Joy to thee, overtowering the knowledge of the wise . . .

For Church Unity

(Catholics During Church Unity Week)

Every January, ending with the Feast of the Conversion of St. Paul on the 25th, the Week of Prayer for Christian Unity is observed. Ecumenical Services are scheduled, and Christians of various Churches or denominations meet for common prayer that, in accordance with Christ's own plea, all might be one in him (Jn 17:20, 21).

We are met to reflect upon the meaning of this week for us.

Pope Paul VI, in his Apostolic Exhortation on evangelization, *Evangelii Nuntiandi* (December 8, 1975), dwells at some length on the link between evangelization—preaching, catechetical instruction, religious education, personal witnessing to the faith—and the ecumenical movement. Disunity among evangelizers can adversely prejudice evangelization.

"The power of evangelization," wrote Pope Paul, "will find itself considerably diminished if those who proclaim the Gospel are divided among themselves in all sorts of ways. Is this not perhaps one of the great sicknesses of evangelization today?"

The subject is apposite to the times. If, the Holy Father argues, the Gospel we preach, teach, or witness to, is viewed as fragmented by doctrinal disputes or bickerings, ideological polarization or mutual anathemas among Christians, how can those to whom the Gospel is communicated fail to be disturbed, disoriented, or even scandalized?

"As evangelizers," Pope Paul explains, "we must offer Christ's faithful not the image of people divided and separated by unedifying quarrels, but the image of a people who are mature in faith and capable of finding a meeting-point beyond the real tensions, thanks to a shared, sincere and disinterested search for truth."

Two theologisms are implicit here. One is the importance of our preaching and witnessing to the same Gospel, without reservation, dilution, or dissent, to men and women desperately hungering for truth.

Thus, the ecumenical movement is retarded, not hastened, when Catholic preachers or teachers—to cite our own world—naively credit the "death of God" fad by mindlessly parroting a mind set or vocabulary which reduces Christianity to nothing but a secularist club, whose premises go no deeper than current sociological and psychological data.

Nor is Church unity helped by those who decline to unite in accordance with the Church's teaching charism regarding urgent moral problems of the times; by an unequivocal rejection of direct abortion, for example.

The second theologism pertains to the manner in which differences of opinion, in matters which are open to discussion, are expressed. Here, mature faith grants the possibility of grey areas. Frequently these problem areas emerge in our all-but-human attempts to apply objective, eternal, truths to entirely new existential problems. But occasionally these grey patches directly touch theology itself.

Unity among Catholics, as well as unity among all Christians, is a way and means of evangelization.

"The Lord's spiritual testament," said Pope Paul VI, "tells us that unity among his followers is not only the proof that we are his, but also the proof that he is sent by the Father. It is the test of the credibility of Christians and of Christ himself . . . Yes, the destiny of evangelization is certainly bound up with the witness of unity given by the Church."

And the witness of unity given by the Church is surely linked with the progress of ecumenism.

For a Jewish/Catholic Gathering

We are met here on the common ground of faith in God. Together we pray the perennial prayer of Deuteronomy, the *Sh'ma*:

Hear, O Israel! The Lord, is our God, the Lord Alone!
Sh'ma Yisrael. Adonai Elohaynu. Adonai Echod. (6:4)

Jesus quoted these words in response to the question, put to him by a scribe: "Which is the first of all the commandments?" (Mk 12:28). Every Saturday evening, in first Vespers of Sunday, every priest and religious bound to pray the Liturgy of the Hours—the official prayer of the Church—rehearses the same prayer:

Hear, O Israel! The Lord is our God, the Lord Alone!

We stand here, then, on these words: we and our Jewish brethren; we stand on this common ground in faith. Here we both refuse to be intimidated by a secularist, materialist world; here we both cry out aloud that at the source of all things, of the heavens and the earth and everything dwelling therein, is the Lord our God, whom we adore, and love, and obey. Here, too, we meet for dialogue, in the effort to bring about a better world.

One way we might implement this meeting is through what one observer, David-Maria Jaeger, has described as "a joint rediscovery of the prophets." Writing in the November 3, 1979 London *Tablet*, he recalled that the prophets literally have spoken for God down through the ages, and their pleadings are still very much relevant.

Yet the same prophetic message constitutes for Christians "the revelatory and theological starting point, or even in a sense the 'outline' and 'prospectus' of the books of the New Testament."

Thus, as the same writer puts it: "Should Christians and Jews not therefore regard their prime purpose in their developing dialogical relationship as being that of 'encouraging each other, for as long as this 'today' lasts, to that constant conversion to the God of justice, mercy and love, which can only be achieved through the constant overcoming of the powerful temptation to isolate religion and its practice from the end, to which they are ordained (and subordinated) as a means, namely perfect union with the just, merciful and loving God of Abraham, Isaac and Jacob, the God and Father of our Lord Jesus Christ.''

We might begin, for example, with Amos, blunt-worded Amos, the earliest of the writing prophets, who reminded his people—and you and me today—that membership in the Covenant entails obligations of social justice. We could dwell together, in prayer, on Scripture's first reference to the dramatic term, ''Day of the Lord,'' and Amos' comforting vision of the remaining small remnant who keep faith (3:12).

An especially apposite prophet we could readily ponder together in these times of confusion, error, and fragmentation, is Jeremiah, highly sensitive and deeply insightful Jeremiah. Remember the prophet's letter to the exiles in Babylon:

''Build houses . . . For I know well the plans I have in mind for you, says the Lord, plans for your welfare, not for woe! plans to give you a future full of hope'' (29:5, 11).

As persons of faith, could not we—Jews and Catholics—meet in strong, common witness against a world which seems to have lost both direction and perspective, a world that seems to turn crazily from the only stable and enduring principles of life and progress?

For common witness to the emptiness and lifelessness of a world without God, we could together reread, and reflect upon, Ezekiel, whose vision of the dry bones comes to mind in the context of T.S. Eliot's *The Waste Land*, generally regarded as one of the most significant poetic statements of the century. Ezekiel's vision can of course help quicken a new spring for our parched earth, the ''Unreal City/Under the brown fog of a winter noon,'' as Eliot paints it. (Eliot, incidentally, was of the opinion that knowledge of the Hebrew tongue was especially profitable for English-speaking persons. See the London *Tablet*, March 10, 1973, p. 232).

Our common belief in Transcendence *can* help strike the rock, as it were, in the midst of our global spritual wasteland, and open up the springs of refreshing, invigorating water, whose ultimate font is the divine Wisdom and Love.

Again, our common commitment is to the Lord, the Lord alone! *Sh'ma Yisrael. Adonai Echod.* Reading the prophets together can help us make this cry heard throughout the world.

PART VI

PARISH OCCASIONS

For the Commissioning of Catechists

At this Eucharist (or ceremony) marking the inauguration of this parish's religious education program this year, all those who have been called to serve as catechists will be formally commissioned.

The significance of this ceremony cannot be overemphasized. What it means is that each of the staff is committing himself or herself to the role of catechist in the name of the Church.

To be a catechist is not simply "to teach religion." Rather, it partakes of a specific ecclesial office, a form of ministry of the word. Which means that the word of the catechist is mysteriously graced by God through the Church.

"The divine word becomes present in catechesis through the human word," the latest (1979) Vatican's General Catechetical Directory explains. "So that it may bear fruit in man and generate inner movements which expel indifference or uncertainty and lead him to embrace the faith, catechesis ought to express the word of God faithfully and present it suitably . . . "

Since catechesis is directed toward faith—toward an acceptance of the living Lord Jesus and his word—it transcends mere presentation of religious data. And whereas it is not quite the same as preaching— through which the graced word is spoken by ordained ministers—it nonetheless mirrors the Church's prophetic mission.

This is why the office of catechist must be carried out in accordance with the Church's magisterium, or its official teaching authority. A catechist's vocation is an ecclesial one; for a catechist to call into question a Church doctrine—the unicity of the Catholic Church, say, or the Real Presence—is a contradiction of this vocation. Again, catechists derive their office not from their own credentials (a Master of Theology degree, say, or an appointment to a faculty), but rather from the Church, through their bishop or pastor.

As the Directory puts it: "The task of catechesis, not an easy one, must be carried out under the guidance of the magisterium of the Church, whose duty it is to safeguard the truth of the divine message, and to watch that the ministry of the word uses appropriate forms of speaking, and prudently considers the help which theological research and the human sciences can give."

Implied herein is the principle that all catechesis must be Christ-ocentric: it must orient to the Father, through Jesus, in the Holy Spirit. Implied, too, is the norm that the ultimate font of all instruction will be the Bible as it is read within the Church.

Implied, too, is loyal adherence to the traditional hierarchy of truths which the Church has always recognized in its historic credal statements, truths which reflect four categories: the mystery of Christ, God-made-man; the mystery of the Holy Spirit, who is present in the Church, sanctifying and guiding it until Jesus comes again as our Savior and Judge; and the mystery of Christ's Mystical Body, the Church, in which Mary the Mother of the Lord has a place of preeminence.

(Here the homilist can bring in the Bible readings of a particular Mass, or accent some points from the readings relevant to catechists.)

The office entrusted to catechists is obviously a noble one, demanding a deep sacramental life, the practice of prayer, and a profound sense of the excellence of the Christian message and its transforming powers.

As we now call these catechists forward, we congratulate them, and pray to God for them.

The Annual Opening Meeting
of a Parish Council

This evening we inaugurate a new year, with a new parish council.

First, as a pastor of this church dedicated to . . . , I congratulate you on your being elected to this council. I convey the congratulations of all the priests of this parish, Father(s) , (as well as the deacons). I join with them all too in a prayer that the living Lord Jesus Christ will grace you in your apostolate here.

If I should ask anything special of you—over and above a strong faith, fraternal charity, and prayer—one request high on the list would be that you try to keep yourselves well informed about the Church and its dynamic life.

The emerging Catholic layperson, and in particular the representative layperson, urgently needs continuing education in the Faith today. Without ready access to the most recent data on the Church, his or her unique contributions in Christian witness will be either inadequate, misleading, or counterproductive.

One of the most practical and effective sources of such data is our diocesan newspaper. Moreover, there are many other magazines and periodicals available; (for example . . .).

The kind of information provided by such journals is an absolute requisite for any role in Christian leadership. Whereas information gaps about the Church can be somewhat bridged by recourse to books and pamphlets, it is through regular reading of Catholic newspapers and periodicals that the Church can best be known, understood and assessed.

Hence, I ask you to commit yourselves to serious reading as a special added responsibility of your membership in our parish council. I assure you that I will be the first among the members of our parish to benefit from the personal updating in the Faith which you assume.

There is no questioning the fact that since Vatican Council II the lay person's role within the Church has expanded substantially, even in unprecedented directions. But the expansion has created a frightening vacuum, in that more responsible areas for action have opened up than there are knowledgeable men or women to enter therein.

Take the case of a parish council asked by the pastor to advise him on matters liturgical. Is every member of the council acquainted with the Constitution on the Sacred Liturgy of Vatican II? With the new Order of Mass, and various recent instructions on the implementation of the liturgy?

Specifically, every now and then one hears of a parish council's asking the pastor to substitute a talk on parish finances, or some other parochial problem, for the Sunday homily. Such a proposal would be inconceivable if the council knew the sacred nature of the homily and the strict liturgical rules governing it.

Again, one occasionally hears of a parish council's making recommendations regarding the curricula in the parish religious education programs without its members' ever having read either the *General Catechetical Directory* (1971) or the *National Catholic Directory for Catholics of the United States*. Both these documents are must reading.

Again, therefore, may I ask you to take up serious reading as a personal obligation, not only for your own welfare, but for that of the entire parish, in view of your new apostolate here in the parish council.

PART VII

SPECIAL GROUPS, NEEDS AND TIMES

For the Dedication of a Church

We are gathered here in prayer and thanksgiving on the occasion of the dedication of this church, named for (the Blessed Virgin Mary or the patron saint or mystery).

Whether a church be a Gothic cathedral towering over a thriving metropolis, or only a small frame chapel on a quaint country road, it is always special, distinguishable from a secular building, regardless of size or style.

Fundamentally, of course, a church's uniqueness stems from its purpose: to be a place for Christian worship. But a church is not merely a place in which to pray; it is itself a prayer. Everything about it serves to elevate the soul Godward: through the senses, the emotions, and eventually, of course, through the intellect and the will, faculties of the soul. Surely this church exemplifies all these characteristics.

The moment we enter this church, for example, we are immediately aware that it is the House of God and the Gate of Heaven. It is the House of God, because the main focal points are the tabernacle of reservation and the altar of sacrifice. At this altar, Jesus' sacrifice on the cross of Calvary is renewed in the Mass, handed down to us by our Lord as the thanksgiving, memorial, sacrificial banquet of the New Testament. Within this tabernacle the Blessed Sacrament is reserved, that Communion might be brought to the sick and the dying in this parish, and that we might worship our divine Lord sacramentally present in the Eucharist in adoration, prayer, and thanksgiving.

This church is also a Gate of Heaven because it is here that we are born to eternal life—through baptism, conferred at the font prominently located here (designate the precise site). Baptism is the doorway to all other sacramental encounters, especially the Eucharist. Here, in this church, too, the Christian is configured to Christ's priesthood in a special way, through Confirmation. Here, cleansing from sin takes place again and again through an encounter with Jesus, the merciful Savior, in the Sacrament of Penance or Reconciliation—confession. It is also here that couples exchange marital vows in Christ—the Sacrament of Matrimony. Finally, it is here that the Mass of Christian Burial is offered.

One truth we should call to mind especially today is that this church is a *church* precisely because it mirrors us, the People of God. Christianity holds that the priestly people gathered for worship, and not the place, constitute the fundamental reality of the concept, "church." St. Paul wrote in Second Corinthians, "*You* are the temple of the living God" (6:16). Even the word "church," which comes to us through the Germanic language from the Greek, originally meant not a place, but the congregation called by Christ. It is only through a happenstance of language development that the "place" of the church came to be called the church.

Fundamentally, *you* are the stained glass, meant to illumine the world with Christ's light and glory. *You* are the aisle, leading others to Christ. *You* are the pulpit, from which the Good News of Christ is proclaimed to a waiting, confused, anxious, erring world. *You* are the altar, upon whom Jesus' work of suffering service is in effect meant to be continued until the end of the world.

For a Charismatic Prayer Group

The Charismatic Prayer Movement, which accents shared prayer—not the same, we know, as praying together—is acknowledged by the Church as endowed with a series of positive qualities. As Pope Paul VI observed in an address at Grottaferrata in October, 1973, this Movement can encourage "the taste for deep prayer, personal and in groups, a return to contemplation and emphasizing of the praise of God, the desire to give oneself completely to Christ, a great availability for the calls of the Holy Spirit, more assiduous reading of the Scripture, generous brotherly devotion, (and) the will to make a contribution to the service of the Church."

"Charismatic," which comes to us from the Greek word for "gift," refers especially to graces by which the Holy Spirit sanctifies and guides the Church. First Corinthians 12:7 reveals the manifestation of the Holy Spirit through such gifts.

Vatican II declared: "These charisms, whether they be the more outstanding or the more simple and widely diffused, are to be received with thanksgiving and consolation for they are especially suited to and useful for the needs of the Church . . ." (Dogmatic Constitution on the Church, no. 12).

The phrase, "needs of the Church," is significant. Charisms are *linked with* the Church; they are given *within the Church*, in unity and charity, and are always in harmony with the Church's teaching. St. Augustine wrote: "We have the Holy Spirit to the extent that we love the Church." Charisms, moreover, witness to Jesus; (read Jn 14:26).

As the National Council of Catholic Bishops' Committee for Pastoral Research and Practices explained in a Statement on Charismatic Renewal in 1975:

Where the Catholic Charismatic movement is making solid progress there is a strongly grounded spirit of faith in Jesus Christ as
Lord. This in turn leads to a renewed interest in prayer, both private
and group prayer. Many of those who belong to the movement
experience a new sense of spiritual values, a heightened conscious-
ness of the action of the Holy Spirit, the praise of God and a
deepening personal commitment to Christ. Many, too, have grown
in devotion to the Eucharist and partake more fruitfully in the
sacramental life of the Church. Reverence for the Mother of the
Lord takes on fresher meaning and many feel a deeper sense of and
attachment to the Church.

The Bishops' statement cautions against the possibility of elitism
(e.g., "a closed circle" which fragments rather than unites in charity), a
false Biblical fundamentalism, neglect of the intellectual and doctrinal
content of the Faith, and reduction of faith merely to a "felt" religious
experience. Moreover, it warns that whereas charisms like healing and
praying in tongues can be genuine manifestations of the Spirit, they
"must be carefully scrutinized" and their importance not exaggerated.

One truth that can help us toward an understanding of the Charismatic
Movement is that the greatest of the charismatics were the saints—
Francis of Assisi, for example, or Martin de Porres, or America's own
Elizabeth Ann Seton. Other obvious examples are Ignatius Loyola,
Teresa of Avila, John of the Cross, Catherine of Siena, Anthony of
Padua, Benedict, and Bernard.

This follows because, as the American bishops have emphasized, the
"greatest authenticating sign of the Spirit" is love, not any kind of love,
but rather that kind of sacrificial, Christian love about which the Apostle
Paul—himself a towering charismatic—wrote in First Corinthians 13:4-
8, 13, in that familiar passage which begins, "Love is patient; love is
kind. . ."

For Priestly and Religious Vocations

Today we are gathered to pray for and to reflect on the need of vocations to the priestly and religious states.

"To pray for," because vocations to the priestly or religious state are faith-invitations. They cannot be understood, much less discussed, without the basic referential axis of belief in the Triune God, who sent his own Son into this world to announce the Good News of Salvation through the sending of the Holy Spirit.

Historian Paul Horgan, whose biography of Archbishop John Baptist Lamy of Santa Fe won the Pulitzer Prize, once described a missionary priest's apostolate in terms of a triangle reaching from heaven to earth. Writing in a short story about early America's great southwest, he describes one of aging Father Louis Bellefontaine's recurring dreams in these moving words:

> . . . a great triangle existed between God in Heaven and any little ranch toward which he rode through the days and himself. It was an always changing triangle, for one of its points was not fixed: his own. As he came nearer and nearer to his goal of the moment, the great hypotenuse between himself and God grew shorter and shorter, until at the last, when he arrived, there was a straight line with all in achieved communion. (*Moments of Truth*, ed. Dan Herr and Joel Wells, Garden City, New York: Doubleday, 1966).

The priest's dream is precisely that of anyone who responds to God's call to priesthood or to the religious life; a call to help abbreviate the hypotenuse of the triangle so as to effect a direct line, as it were, between heaven and one's place on earth.

Priests are called to accomplish this primarily through preaching, by gathering believers into eucharistic celebration, and by leading the world to God's grace through sacramental encounter, beginning in baptism.

The priestly vocation is given as a personal call by the Lord Jesus himself. Because the Lord's wisdom cannot be questioned, and because the Lord graces whomever he calls, a vocation to the priesthood can—in Pope John Paul II's words to the priests of Philadelphia on October 4, 1979—be answered affirmatively "with utmost confidence and without reservation." In fact, the call itself is a grace.

Religious consecration by vows in an Order or congregation, such as that made by sisters, nuns, brothers and monks, likewise reflects a personal invitation by Christ. Hence the call to religious life is also a grace in itself. The essence of this call, as John Paul II reminded women religious in Washington, D.C., on October 7, 1979, is "to profess within and for the benefit of the Church, poverty, chastity and obedience in response to God's special invitation, in order to praise and serve God in greater freedom of heart . . . and to have one's life more closely conformed to Christ in the manner of life chosen by him and his blessed Mother."

As a commitment to Christ, religious life is also a commitment to Christ's Body, the Church. Hence it is a service to the Church, a Yes of Consent to join in various ways of the apostolate, which, again, can be described as shortening the hypotenuse of the triangle between heaven and one specific place on earth.

"Your service in the Church," Pope John Paul reminded the sisters—and, of course, all in vows—is "an extension of Christ to whom you have dedicated your life. For it is not yourself you put forward, but Christ Jesus as Lord. Like John the Baptist . . . your life must be characterized by a complete availability: a readiness to serve as the needs of the Church require . . ."

These are beautiful invitations: priestly and religious vocations. We pray for all those today who have received such calls and strive daily to keep responding to them in unreserved faith, hope, and love. And we pray that young people may so open their hearts to the call to priesthood or religious life that they will remain alert, with anxious expectation, to the possibility of God's calling them personally to one of these states of life.

For Reverence for Life (Direct Abortion)

We are gathered for a liturgy (or service) celebrating life, which we revere as a sacred gift from our all-holy God. As Pope John Paul II said in his final Mass on the Mall in Washington, D.C., on Sunday, October 8, 1979:

"Human life is precious because it is the gift of a God whose love is infinite, and when God gives life, it is forever."

Earlier in 1979, during his pilgrimage to his native Poland, the Holy Father said:

"If a person's right to life is violated at the moment in which he is first conceived in his mother's womb, an indirect blow is struck also at the whole of the moral order, which serves to ensure the inviolable goods of man."

"Among those goods, life occupies the first place.

"The Church defends the right to life, not only in regard to the majesty of the Creator, who is the first giver of this life, but also in respect of the essential good of the human person."

The awesome sanctity of human life is heralded time and time again in the Scriptures. There we are told that life is oriented toward eternity, that death itself is absorbed by life (2 Cor 4:10, 5:4; 1 Cor 15:35-55).

Further, Jesus literally identifies with life. In 1 John 1:1, he is viewed as the "Word of life," and in John 14:16, he describes himself as "the way, the truth, and the life."

Human life, we believe, is precious from the time of conception. At the end of the first century, the *Didache*, one of the Church's earliest catechetical manuals, taught:

"Now, the way of life is this: first, love the God who made you; secondly, your neighbor as yourself; do not do to another what you do not wish to be done to yourself ... Do not murder; do not commit adultery, ... do not kill a fetus by abortion or commit infanticide ... Hate no man..."

This earliest catechetical admonition about the sacredness of life within the womb is set forth in a context of love. A key dimension of God's life is love; to attack human life at any point, is to contradict God's love.

Human life, again, is sacred; all human life, from the time of conception. Direct abortion is evil, and must be repudiated.

The holiness of human life, Pope John Paul has insisted, rests on the uniqueness of every person as a creature of God called to be a brother or sister of Christ by reason of the Incarnation or Redemption—called to God's life in God's love, therefore. This is why we as Catholics celebrate human life against every influence or action that threatens or weakens it, and help make every life more human in all its dimensions.

This is why, too, that we must stand up whenever human life is threatened, and "proclaim that no one ever has the authority to destroy life" (General Audience of January 3, 1979).

Part of the problem with those who do not stand up against abortion today, it seems, is moral blindness; concretely, a strange refusal or inability to recognize evil for evil, and to understand that *evil can never be good*.

One of the Gospels dramatically attesting to this truth is the story of Jesus' being slandered with the accusation that he worked miracles only through the power of the Prince of Devils (Lk 11:14-28). The way that abortion is defended today reminds one of such an effort to erase the very clear line distinguishing evil from good. This effort is a lie, consonant with the Father of Lies. Abortion is a lie.

For Christian Teachers

By and large, the teaching profession in this nation today is not always accorded the esteem which by its nature it merits.

There are many complex reasons for this. Instead of attempting to detail or to discuss these causes, I should like only to state a positive thesis in view of the disturbing fact. Namely, that if anything can profit the teaching profession today it is: (1) a profound conviction on the part of each teacher of the nobility of his or her vocation, and (2) a day-to-day implementation of this conviction.

What I mean is that teaching is possessed of a nobility all its own. So much is evident from its very definition: i.e., the deliberate and systematic influence exerted upon the immature, through instruction, discipline, and the harmonious development of all the powers of the person—physical, aesthetic, social, intellectual and spiritual—in accordance with their essential hierarchy of importance, by and for their individual uses, and directed toward the union of the educand with his Creator and Final End.

Teaching entails far more than simple indoctrination. It means helping others grow to a realization of their *raison d' etre*—in the words of the catechism: to know, love, and serve God in this life, and to be happy with him forever in the next. In the Christian context, therefore, teaching is synonymous with immediately participating in the formation of Christlike adults. It is as noble as this.

Possessed of such a conviction, a teacher ought to implement it as best he or she can. Specifically, there are several virtues—the "teacher's virtues"—which the teacher must not only cultivate but also exemplify.

Charity is important above all else. To the teacher, all pupils without exception must be viewed as brother-children in Christ, for whom the

Precious Blood was shed in the Redemptive Act of Calvary. It matters not what the color of their skin, what their racial or national lineage, what their so-called native intelligence or aptitude.

Justice is the second "teacher's virtue"—that special quality commonly described by students as "fairness." Justice implies a scrupulous rejection of deliberate prejudice, and objectivity in grading.

Unselfishness is another "must" virtue for teaching. The moment the teacher gives the impression that he or she doesn't have time for a student reasonably asking for assistance merely because, for instance, aiding the student can't enhance his or her professional prestige, the teacher betrays his or her vocation.

And then there is humility. The arrogant teacher sets a wall between himself or herself and the class, hence defeats the very purpose for which he or she has been engaged. Too, doesn't it occasionally happen that a pupil, though less educated in the formal sense than the teacher, is nevertheless gifted with considerably higher intellectual ability? If a teacher "fights" this fact through pride, can't the circumstances be sensed by a class? Hubris must be discarded.

Teachers should manifest an intense love for truth, which means that they should not only strive to be masters of their subjects, but that they should never hesitate to accept a fact over an hypothesis (especially when fact contradicts hypothesis).

There is need, finally, for teachers to profess the nobility of their calling. Certainly they should not be among those who habitually detract from it. And they should try to encourage youths of the highest calibre to enter the ranks they serve so well.

Teaching is, in a sense, a ministry.

For a High School Commencement (Girls)

There is a clever one-act play by the English writer James Barrie, the same Barrie who gave us *Peter Pan*. This one-act play is entitled, *The Twelve Pound Look*, and it is especially important for women. It doesn't have to do with dieting, however. "Twelve Pound" here refers to British currency; what we call "dollars," the British call "pounds."

In Sir James Barrie's time—just after the turn of this century—twelve pounds was the price of a typewriter in England. And, to make a long story short, the typewriter, which had only recently been invented, provided women with a dramatic new means toward making their own livelihood in a professional status. In one sense, owning a typewriter then was liberating; with twelve pounds a woman could achieve a degree of unprecedented status, acquire a professional position, and, if she chose to, finance her own way through secondary school—high school—and even beyond.

In one way, then, Barrie's *The Twelve Pound Look* focuses on how the typewriter helped provide women with an economic key by which they could enlarge upon their options in the areas of personal and professional fulfillment.

A sound high school education is designed to do the same. If it is true that one's chances of finding employment today are usually related at least to one's basic education, it is also true that one's opportunities in general in this world frequently increase in accordance with one's education. (By "opportunities" here I mean all kinds, including the prospect of marriage. One comedian, speaking at the graduation of a Catholic girls' high school near Los Angeles, and not too far from a Catholic boys' high, reminded the young ladies not to lose sight of the many "opportunities" awaiting them. By "opportunities," *he* meant the 200 boys graduating at the nearby school).

Besides amplifying one's options toward fulfillment, a sound education, like strong faith in God, also ensures better perspectives with which to view the world. The more educated we become, the more we tend to realize our role and responsibility in society, and, consequently, how we may better contribute to the social structure. Likewise, schooling helps us recognize our present limitations. In mathematical language, you might say that education provides us with an "axis of coordinates."

Take an example. Remember the first astronaut to float free in space? One of the most serious problems he had to solve was how to find a point of reference so that he could determine his position at any given moment. You know how it is within a closed-in elevator. If there were no floor indicators (lights) on the panel, you could hardly know whether you were ascending or descending. To determine the direction of your motion, you would have to see some other point outside the elevator. The astronaut chose the sun as his point of reference. He couldn't have selected the earth, since while he was in orbit the earth was continuously changing positions in relation to him and to the space capsule to which he was tethered.

As the sun represented one point of the axis in the case of the astronaut, so the basic education you have acquired can be a point of reference for your position in the world. It was well worth your effort.

For Thanksgiving Day

Thanksgiving Day is America's own religious holiday. Religious? Unquestionably so. To whom is thanksgiving rendered on this day? To God, of course. And religion is defined—the Roman orator Cicero's definition has perdured through the ages—in terms of man's links with God. Acknowledgement of God and religious response are integral to our annual Thanksgiving observance.

Historically, religious faith was also at Thanksgiving's origins. One of the reasons for the first Thanksgiving festival of 1621 was—as *Mourt's Relation* puts it—to rejoice over the plentiful harvest made possible ''by the goodnesse (*sic*) of God.''

Later, in the Plymouth Colony Thanksgiving Proclamation of 1668—really the first official document of its kind—God's bounty is explicitly affirmed as the cause for celebration.

One curious sidelight, insofar as the religious aspect of the first Thanksgiving Day is concerned, is its remote relationship to Martinmas, St. Martin's Day, a medieval harvest festival which was still celebrated in Holland around the time the Pilgrims sailed. It is interesting to note that when the Plymouth colonists decided to have their first ''Thanksgiving'' festival, they sent hunters after wild geese (the goose was the mainstay of the St. Martin's Day Dinner) and drank a toast from the first wine of the grape harvest, a traditional Martinmas ritual. (Fortunately for us, the hunters came back with a few turkeys as well as the geese, although one wonders how they could have taken any game with those flared-muzzle blunderbusses).

George Washington, our first President, proclaimed a Thanksgiving Day on at least two (perhaps several) occasions. However, the observance as we know it—an annual national observance with religious overtones—did not arrive until Civil War times.

It was Abraham Lincoln who assigned the fourth Thursday in November as a national Thanksgiving Day, specifically that God might be thanked for his benedictions upon the land.

We have a traditional hymn:

> Now thank we all our God
> With heart and hands and voices . . .

Surely this is the key theme we are asked to keep in mind on Thanksgiving Day. We are united to thank the Lord for all his blessings: to be alive today, in this challenging era; to be chosen to be a member of the Church now, in these exciting times; to have been blessed with grace in so many ways, including the very special persons we have known in our lives who have literally helped us change our lives more meaningfully in Christian discipleship; for our health; and for so much more. This is a day for explicitly counting our blessings.

At the same time, Thanksgiving Day is a dramatic reminder to the effect that America's roots *are* religious; that our Founding Fathers were intensely aware of God's presence, and of God's providence, *precisely in their colonial existence.*

The Puritans believed—as the hymn sings—that God

> Has blessed us on our way
> with countless gifts of love
> And still is ours today.